MOTIVES AND MECHANISMS

MOTIVES AND

An introduction to
the psychology of action

MECHANISMS

Rom Harré, David Clarke
and Nicola De Carlo

METHUEN · LONDON AND NEW YORK

First published in 1985 by
Methuen & Co. Ltd
11 New Fetter Lane, London
EC4P 4EE

Published in the USA by
Methuen & Co.
in association with Methuen, Inc.
733 Third Avenue, New York,
NY 10017

Typeset by Rowland
Phototypesetting Ltd,
Bury St Edmunds, Suffolk
Printed in Great Britain by Richard
Clay (The Chaucer Press), Bungay,
Suffolk

British Library Cataloguing in
Publication Data

Harré, Rom
Motives and mechanisms: an
introduction to the psychology of
action.
1. Act (Philosophy)
I. Title II. Clarke, David
III. De Carlo, Nicola
128'.4 BF789.A/

ISBN 0-416-36230-3
ISBN 0-416-36240-0 Pbk

Library of Congress Cataloging in
Publication Data

Harré, Rom.
Motives and mechanisms.
Bibliography: p.
Includes indexes.
1. Intentionalism.
2. Motivation (Psychology)
I. Clarke, David, R.N.M.S.
II. De Carlo, Nicola.
III. Title. [DNLM: 1. Motivation.
2. Psychology. BF 503 H296m]
BF619.5.H37 1985 150'.1
84-22730

ISBN 0-416-36230-3
ISBN 0-416-36240-0 (pbk.)

CONTENTS

LIST OF FIGURES

PREFACE

'Action' – that is, intended human behaviour in specific social and physical settings – has recently become the focus of a new style of theoretical and empirical psychology. A considerable literature has accumulated at advanced levels. There have been substantial theoretical monographs like John Shotter's *Social Accountability and Selfhood* (1984) and detailed reports of comprehensive empirical studies like Marga Kreckel's *Communicative Acts and Shared Knowledge in Natural Discourse* (1981). Most of this work is highly technical and not suitable for undergraduate courses devoted to introducing the new ideas and techniques. There is a particular problem for those who work in academic departments still dominated by old-fashioned empiricist philosophies of science. In this work we have tried to present the main lines of 'new wave' psychological thinking as both contrasting with and complementary to recent orthodoxy.

To read this book successfully one must bear in mind that new approaches to theory and method of enquiry in some well-established scientific field are often made more difficult by a natural and persistent tendency to understand the new ideas in terms of the old ways. It is important to realize that the approach that we have chosen to call 'the psychology of action', but which goes under other names too, is not just a revision or modification of old ways of doing psychology but a radically different approach to the understanding of human behaviour. It is not just an additional theory inserted into existing psychology but a thoroughgoing alternative to it. Seen from the new view a human mind does not emerge out of processes internal to the human individual. It is a shaping of the activities of the whole person, including their brain and nervous system, by socio-linguistic influences. In the course of this shaping a person acquires a fragment of the rules and conventions of their society, in accordance with which they form projects for action and choose the means for realizing those projects.

The change to a radically new perspective on the problems of understanding human thought and action, human emotions and the forms of human lives, is not just a matter of abandoning a bad scientific theory and taking up a better one. It involves the realization that psychology is intimately bound up with the moral and political assumptions that people unknowingly bring to every task they approach, particularly those in which human beings are involved as objects of action or study.

Our first task in this book is to try to make clear the very deep-seated scientific errors and complementary moral and political assumptions that are embedded in contemporary psychology. A person's moral and political beliefs may seem to them to be of universal validity, but from a scientific point of view we must keep always before us the fact that these beliefs shape our conception of ourselves and of our fellow human beings on a very local scale. Psychology cannot be a science based on the discovery of causes and their effects, nor can its best work have any special claim to univer-sality. The task of psychology, as a science, must, then, be the attempt to find out the systems of tacit rules and conventions that are followed in the creation of everyday life. Those rules and conven-tions make a sort of 'middle level' of the three tiers of processes within which human life is embedded. At a lower level are the kind of automatic microprocesses with which our plans are executed and our rule-governed actions actually brought off. These are the proper sphere of cognitive psychology. The middle level, to which we have already alluded in some detail, is the playground for the ethogenic method, where we try to find out what bodies of social, linguistic, practical and other kinds of knowledge are typical of persons of various kinds and competences. But there is a third level, or tier of structures and processes, which is as remote from conscious experience as the microprocessors by which we see, move, speak and so on. This is the level of collective processes and structures, which are social in the larger sense. The most important of these, we believe, are the multiple moral orders that enter in one way or another into every aspect of our lives, and most particularly into the formation of our culturally distinctive emotions.

This work has been conceived as an introduction to the psychology of action. It is not an introduction to psychology. Like any other science, psychology is part of a historical process, and what we suggest by way of innovation today no doubt bears somewhere within it the seeds of the movement that will in turn replace it. For the foreseeable future it seems likely, for all sorts of institutional and political reasons, that much of the existing syllabus of traditional psychology will continue to be taught in universities and colleges. For those who want to know the limitations of that point of view we offer this brief account of the new one. But, just as it would be impossible to understand quantum mechanics without a background in classical physics, so much that we put forward in this book will make sense only to those who have already struggled with, and come to feel the need for, reform in the existing framework.

We begin our argument with a fairly detailed discussion of the shortcomings of the existing 'paradigm'. This leads us into a brief introduction to the idea of a psychology of three tiers, only one of which is open to conscious awareness. To go further we need to know how explanatory sciences work. It becomes clear, then, that alone amongst current branches of psychology cognitive psychology is a genuinely explanatory science. However, as conceived it is incapable of tackling certain central questions of psychology. We need something more, and we find this in the form of various new methods of enquiry which emphasize the power of ordinary language and the authority of ordinary actors. These new methods do not wholly exclude traditional techniques, though, and for some preliminary investigations we show that they can still play an important role. Finally, to illustrate the sorts of issues that can be tackled through the new ways of studying human beings, we describe, in some detail, how a 'new psychologist' would undertake the study of the emotions and of personality. We are particularly grateful to Charles Antaki for many helpful criticisms of an early draft.

Oxford and Padua, 1984   ROM HARRÉ
                                                          DAVID CLARKE
                                                          NICOLA DE CARLO

1 WHY DO WE NEED A 'NEW PSYCHOLOGY'?

In this book we shall try to explain why much of contemporary psychology is unsatisfactory. We shall offer an alternative, an approach that, we hope, will help to overcome some of the difficulties to which we draw attention and at the same time will preserve the real advances that have been made by academic psychology. However, one might object, are there not already a great many 'psychologies' available? Even in this century we have had associationism, the remnants of classical behaviourism, the gestalt approach, psychodynamics and more recently cognitive psychology (see Margolis 1984). Why do we need yet another '-ism' or '-ology'? There are many people who would go further. Since we already have many ways to understand the human heart and mind – literature, history, ethics, logic, jurisprudence and anthropology, for instance – why do we need psychology at all? Neither of these questions can be answered in a phrase, but we hope that by the end of this study they will have been adequately dealt with. There is a place for a scientific study of thought, feeling and action, but for a variety of reasons none of the existing attempts to create such a study has succeeded or, indeed, could succeed.

We begin with a discussion of the limitations of much contemporary psychology, scientism, individualism, universalism and causalism. This leads us into an examination of the relation between psychology and the natural sciences on the one hand, and psychology and common sense on the other. We show how the relation between academic psychology and the ordinary means by which human beings manage their daily lives is different from the relation between the natural sciences and common sense. Common sense must be incorporated into, and not superseded by, scientific psychology, since it is the system by which one important level of human action is managed.

Some problems of contemporary psychology

Our first task will be to set out four main vices to which we believe contemporary psychology is particularly prone. They are: *scientism*, the use of a misleading vocabulary and associated methods of enquiry drawn mainly from the physical sciences; *individualism*, the assumption that each person is a psychological unit in which all important processes occur; *universalism*, the tendency to report the results of studies of the people of one's own 'tribe' as if these results were true of all mankind; *causalism*, the attempt to explain all psychological phenomena as the effects of causes. Discussion of these problems leads us to examine the relation of psychology to the biological sciences on the one hand and to common sense on the other. Psychology is not a branch of the natural sciences, though the mechanisms of the production of thought, feeling and action in human beings are at least in part physiological. Nor can psychology ignore common sense, since it is in accordance with commonsense principles and understandings that we live. Yet there can be a scientific psychology which is something more than organized common sense.

Broadly speaking, we have three 'psychologies' in play in contemporary western Europe and North America. There is the cluster of sometimes incompatible theories and practices used by psychiatrists, social workers and others who deal with various kinds of personal disturbances and miseries. Then there is the laboratory-dominated but highly volatile 'academic' psychology of the universities. Finally there are the unofficial doctrines of the fringe psychologies which dominate the popular imagination and which still have strong connections with religion and magic. These three are set against the background of daily life, where the forces implicit in ordinary language and material practices shape our thoughts and feelings into the forms permitted by our local culture.

This book is about academic psychology and its relation to the languages and practices of everyday life. In this chapter we hope to bring out some of the reservations and doubts that have emerged as criticisms of much of contemporary academic psychology have mounted. In the end we hope to have made clear why yet another 'new psychology' must be promoted to redress some of the more obvious errors of the immediate past.

The tendency to scientism

Much of the style of recent psychology has come from a self-conscious attempt by psychologists to borrow from the methods – or rather from what they took to be the methods – of the physical and biological sciences. We shall call the effect of this influence on the activities of psychologists *scientism*. It appears not only in the adoption of certain methods of enquiry but also in the use of a characteristic vocabulary borrowed from the physical sciences. For example, the use of such terms as 'measure' or 'variable' for talking about emotions, attitudes, friendship, and so on, is a case of scientism. In the physical sciences these terms have a well-established usage that is closely related to the techniques of experiment and the use of mathematics to represent physical laws. It is by no means obvious that the appropriate conditions for valid usage are well established in psychology.

A scientistic vocabulary usually appears in the first instance as a replacement for a set of common English terms (and to a lesser extent French and German ones). These terms are in everyday use for expressing our working psychological judgements and theories. In a scientistic transformation of this vocabulary 'affect' is used instead of 'feeling' and/or 'emotion', 'helping behaviour' instead of 'helping', and so on. Scientism in psychology has two opposite but unfortunately non-cancelling effects. Sometimes all the nuances of the ordinary-language terms which the scientistic terms have replaced are carried over into psychology, including ambiguities. Just as the term 'help' covers both aid (assisting someone who is competent in some measure to tackle a job) and succour (assistance for someone who is incapable of managing at all), so it seems from the literature does the term 'helping behaviour'. But, whereas in ordinary language the distinction between these species of helping is incorporated in the semantic rules for the use of the term 'help', there are no given semantic rules for the neologism 'helping behaviour'. Not only is it ambiguous, like 'help', but we are not even sure how the ambiguities are to be resolved. On the other hand, there may be a gross impoverishment caused by such a substitution of terms. 'Affect' seems to be used both for 'emotion' and for 'feeling', and these are not synonyms in English. If we have only the term 'affect', we may find – as indeed has occurred in academic psychology – that the important distinction between emotion and feeling has been mislaid.

Furthermore, there may be serious inaccuracies in the implications of a word which was introduced as a scientistic substitute for an English term for describing the psychology of another culture. The vocabulary of a foreign language never exactly matches that of the language of academic psychology, scientistic English. The way the apparently corresponding terms of a foreign language are used reflects features of the psychology of that culture. Cross-cultural displacement of terms must take account of the fact that psychological phenomena in the exotic culture usually resemble the phenomena of Anglo-American mental life only in some respects. For instance, it is part of the logical grammar of emotion words in English that they can properly be applied to someone who is solitary. It seems that this feature of grammar reflects a psychological phenomenon of western culture that is not found among Eskimos: emotion terms are applied to people only when they are with others. Therefore, to use the term 'affect' of Eskimos can subtly influence the psychological hypotheses about them. It may suggest that the communality of Eskimo emotion is somehow a 'repression' of individual or 'natural' emotion; but there may be no 'natural' human emotions among Eskimos or anyone else. Heelas (Heelas and Lock 1981) has gone so far as to suggest that it may be misleading to use the term 'emotion' or any of its scientistic substitutes for describing the way certain peoples manage their feelings, since they may deal with them in ways that involve cognitive and social processes very different from ours.

Ironically, scientistic terminology tends to perpetuate the assumptions of commonsense psychology by eliminating those terms that, if carefully analysed, would reveal those assumptions. Sometimes there are features of the use of commonsense terms that are of great importance to a truly scientific psychology. For instance, if we preserve the commonsense vocabulary for identifying and classifying the emotions, we can quickly become aware of how far moral assessments enter into the emotions we feel. The emotion of anger is not just a worked-up feeling; it also involves the moral assessment of that which has made us angry. We are angry when our adrenalin has been set flowing by some event we regard as a transgression of our rights, status, and so on. The fact that we do not get angry with our dentist for hurting us can be explained by the fact that we do not regard it as any kind of morally reprehensible interference. We make over to our dentist certain rights to interfere with us in ways that would be unacceptable from others.

Scientism is not just a matter of borrowing a vocabulary from the physical sciences; it may also involve taking over methods or techniques of enquiry that have grown up in the sciences of inanimate nature. The most obvious borrowing has been that of the technique of experiment, which has sometimes been advocated as the exclusive method of empirical enquiry. We shall be discussing the problems that beset the old psychology on account of this in Chapter 6.

Finally, we must note yet another effect of the use of scientistic vocabulary as rhetoric in psychology. Ordinary-language terms bring with them a great variety of implicit theories about how this or that kind of action is produced. These theories range from explanations in terms of habits, where personal agency is at a minimum, through to those which, by using action terms and mentioning intentions, encourage us to see what people do as explicit acts of reasoning and judgement. The distinction between a science that sees what people do as actions based upon beliefs and intentions and a science that sees what people do as behaviour caused by a stimulus will emerge ever more strongly as we proceed. The trouble with scientism is that it leads us to adopt the second of these versions of psychology without a thorough examination of the propriety of abandoning the first.

In order to reject scientism, it will be necessary to show that the tacit presuppositions that slip in with the borrowed vocabulary are at best over-restrictive and at worst false. To test these presuppositions we must always be willing to turn to other cultures to check our results, though that is not always easy. By slipping into an apparently 'neutral' scientific vocabulary, scientists can slide into ethnocentrism – the fallacy of supposing that what is typical of their own culture is typical of all mankind.

However, one cannot just uncritically adopt ordinary language as the technical vocabulary for a truly scientific psychology. Though the phenomena of the mental life are defined by the ordinary languages of mankind, it is by no means the case that the processes by which those phenomena are produced can always be dealt with in the same way. In Chapter 2 we shall explain why a scientific psychology must invoke processes of which the actors are unaware, at least in the course of the action, some of which are social and some of which are individual. Just as do the physical sciences, psychology must make use of analogical reasoning and metaphorical developments of language to find ways of describing those processes which the actors, for one reason or another, cannot observe.

Individualism

A second feature of contemporary psychology, more influential even than scientism, is a general assumption of individualism: the tendency to assume that the subject matter of psychology is individual thought and action; that cognitive processes like remembering and reasoning can occur only in individuals. Typically, experimenters require each subject to perform their allotted tasks by themselves. For example, in moral-developmental psychology the subjects are *each* asked to write out a solution to a moral dilemma – for example, the problems for the boy Heinz, who is torn between family loyalty and obedience to the law. Then the answers are analysed one by one and, depending on the satisfaction of various criteria, the *individuals* who took part are each assigned to levels of moral development: conventional, post-conventional, and so on. But this technique, which seems to echo that of the school examination, presupposes that moral reasoning is typically performed by each individual separately. In fact, as we all know, most moral decisions are made in the course of conversations, discussions about what should or should not be done, or perhaps what is and what is not one's duty. Moral reasoning is, more often than not, a collective activity. In psychology generally, we must take account of the fact that remembering, reasoning and expressing emotions are part of the life of institutions, of structured, self-regulating groups, such as armies, monasteries, schools, families, businesses and factories.

Can a universal psychology be assumed?

Most of the psychological experiments that have ever been performed have used British or American college students as subjects.
The results of such experiments have been published as if they were
comparable to those achieved in the physical sciences. Yet there is
good reason to think that we cannot assume that the ways in which
such young people think and act are universal features of the
psychology of all mankind. Anthropological research suggests that
there may be very different ways of thought among peoples else-
where. For example, the work of anthropologists such as Catherine
Lutz (1981) shows how diverse are the repertoires of human emotions characteristic of different cultures. We shall look in detail at the
psychology of the emotions in Chapter 7. There is also evidence that
even so basic a psychological phenomenon as the perception of space
and time and the way people reason about spatial and temporal
problems may not be the same everywhere.

It seems reasonable to suppose that all human infants are born
with much the same potential (those differences in intellect, personality and style that seem to loom so large are minuscule when
compared with how human beings differ from their closest primate
relatives). Many features of human psychology will be universal. If
there are differences in the psychologies of different tribes, they must
therefore arise from different 'schedules' by which infants are transformed into the kind of people that a culture favours. One way of
testing the hypothesis that the differences in behaviour, in thought
patterns and in moral assumptions in various cultures are deep
enough to be reckoned differences in 'psychology' would be to make
a very careful comparison between the ways in which people are
'manufactured'. It may even be the case that different cultures, by
emphasizing one sort of emotion rather than another, may produce
people whose physiological systems differ one from another. There
are cultures that encourage fear in the face of danger, others that try
to suppress it. This is certainly true of human anatomy, where
different cultural conventions covering diet and exercise can cause
people, originally of the same stock, to have very different physiques.

Above all, however, the differences in human language might be
examined for the sources of differences in the psychologies of
mankind. It was thought at one time that language determined
thought, so that the absence of a certain word precluded the formation of a corresponding thought. This was the Sapir–Whorf hypoth-

esis, which is now generally agreed to be much exaggerated. Common experience with our own language is enough to prove that the limits of what can be expressed are not fixed by vocabulary. We can formulate a new thought in more roundabout ways. The Eskimo language, Intuit, has a great many words for 'snow', each picking out a different variety; but those varieties can easily be conveyed in English by using descriptive phrases. In this book we shall be making use of a much weaker hypothesis about the relation between language and thought. The linguistic resources available to a thinker facilitate some ways of thinking rather than others. We shall follow Vygotsky (1962) in adopting the idea that the learning of language 'shapes' the mind so that thought and feeling become organized in ways that are specific to and characteristic of each major human culture.

Despite our emphasis on the need to take into account the possibility of there being very local 'psychologies', much of our psychology must respect the general conditions of human life, some certainly set by our biological nature and the kind of environment within which the human race has developed. It would be very surprising indeed if these conditions were not reflected in some general features of human psychology, the most obvious of which would be in the psychology of perception. The work of child psychologists such as Tom Bower (1982) and Jerome Bruner (1972) has shown how sophisticated are the perceptual abilities of new-born babies; for example, an 8-hour-old baby can imitate its mother's facial expressions. Yet some apparently obvious universals of human thought turn out to be rather local. It would seem obvious to people like ourselves that there must be a universal distinction between the psychologies of children and of adults, but this is not so. The idea that children should be treated as if their modes of reasoning, their repertoire of emotions and their capacity to make moral judgements were different from those of adults is a very recent innovation. According to the French historian Ariès it is scarcely 300 years old (see Ariès 1962).

Perhaps the most famous universalistic theory in psychology has been Noam Chomsky's view that all human languages have a common basic syntactic structure. Most linguists would now regard this theory as mistaken, seeing syntax as a cultural phenomenon, perhaps even as inessential to the basic forms of language (see Harris 1980). There have been many other theories based upon universalistic hypotheses. The anthropologist Claude Lévi-Strauss (1968) made a very subtle and persistent effort to demonstrate that there were basic thought forms, built up on binary classifications, such as raw/cooked, honey/ashes, etc. These could be transformed in various ways to appear in all sorts of features of a culture, including myths and systems of classification. At this moment in the developing history of psychology there is a tendency to emphasize the local and historically ephemeral aspects of human thought and feeling, and to play down universals. We shall try to strike a balance between an emphasis on the unique character of local thought patterns and an uncritical tendency to universalize the results of very restricted investigations.

Are psychological phenomena the effects of causes?

When a volcano erupts, vulcanologists explain the event by reference to a chain of causes. Water seeps down through cracks in the rocks to the hot interior of the earth and is there converted to steam; an enormous pressure builds up and is released by an explosion. A geyser is a kind of mini-eruption. The mountain is a mere passive component in the 'mechanism' of an eruption. The physical sciences are causal sciences. They seek to explain the events that occur in the physical world and the natures of physical things by reference to causes. Except in the most recondite branches of physics, causes are deterministic. When the conditions are right, each step in the chain of causes and effects leads inexorably to the next. Causal mechanisms in the physical world seem to be characteristically different from the mental processes which underlie thought and action, and which are involved in how we interpret our feelings. At first sight one would think that a great deal of effort would be put into exploring the similarities and differences between the causality typical of physical processes and the ways people manage their actions, develop their thoughts and display their emotions. But psychology has not developed like that. By jumping into a scientistic way of speaking (perhaps in the first instance merely to take a stand for a scientific rather than a literary or historical approach to the problems of understanding the human mind) much of modern psychology has simply assumed that the causal form of explanation is the right one.

There is a very great difference between the workings of simple causal mechanisms and the way human beings act. Human beings can reflect on their actions, can decide that some plan or project is leading into trouble and can set about recovering themselves. Human beings' actions are typically performed *in accordance with* rules rather than *determined by* causes. Sometimes, of course, we would want to say that what a person did was determined by a cause, but those are the sorts of cases where we would speak of obsessional behaviour, and even madness. The issue of whether we should think of people as self-determining agents or as complex causal mechanisms has sometimes been confused with the distinction between mentalism and materialism. The very word-processor upon which the text of this book has been prepared is a sophisticated machine, capable of some of the actions of self-monitoring and self-correction that we would once have assumed could be performed only by human beings. This particular machine (blessed with a mere 128K of 'mind') only mimics a few human capacities, but it does have some of the hierarchical organization of the mind. Perhaps future developments will produce machines with such capacities that we might want to say that they truly think (and perhaps even feel). In that case it would be just as misguided to study them by means of the simple causal approach to behaviour as it is to study people in that way. Yet we shall find that there are many fields of psychology – including, most surprising of all, the field of social psychology – where the scientistic rhetoric that psychologists have adopted has led them to take for granted that a form of behaviour can be explained in terms of sets of simple cause–effect relationships, typical of simple systems like volcanoes. Is there, in fact, a real difference between causal and non-causal theories? Perhaps we should treat decisions, plans, and so on, as a special category of causes. The difference has to do with the actor's relation to the 'program' of his or her action. A real actor could have done otherwise. But when we are thinking in causal terms of what the actor did it seems difficult, if not impossible, to justify that important qualification. Such a qualification has the further consequence of leading us to think of what the actor did (or didn't do) in moral terms. The old psychology tried to study human action within a causal order, while the new psychology tries to reach a scientific understanding of human life within a moral order or orders.

Why, then, do people use rhetorics? Why are they not content with that most subtle and expressive of all intellectual instruments, particularly where psychological matters are concerned: ordinary language? Language is not only a device for passing on information, setting out plans and projects, and so on. It is also a medium through which people display their worth, publicly express the sort of person they wish to be taken to be. We are all familiar with the special ways in which politicians, trade-union leaders, military spokesmen and other experts speak. Each has a characteristic rhetoric. Scientists are no exception. A certain sort of language is called for by the conventions in use among the members of the community. Here is a psychologist talking about how the ideal of fairness (a moral ideal in our sort of society) and the tendency of people to favour their own kind can be used to define and study different kinds of discrimination:

> Intergroup discrimination is probably best conceptualized as a psychological or behavioural continuum which varies from maximal ingroup favouritism at one pole to exact fairness at the other (or through fairness as the midpoint to A or outgroup favouritism at the opposite pole).

Leaving aside the very odd disjunction 'psychological or behavioural', we seem to have a very reasonable definition of discrimination; at least it is an intelligible proposal which could be used in a practical study. Unfortunately, scientism takes over, and the author proceeds as follows:

> Any specific behavioural tendency or position on this continuum would be reflected in both F and FAV pulls. A perfect correspondence between conceptual variables and operational measures would be as follows: maximal FAV and minimal F would indicate maximum discrimination, minimal FAV and maximal F exact fairness and so on. . . . The important point of this simple analysis is that in half the possible combinations of F and FAV values, the pull of F will be greater than FAV and yet the subjects will nevertheless be discriminating in favour of the ingroup over the outgroup. (Turner 1980)

Notice how the choice of a scientistic rhetoric of 'F and FAV pulls' comes to dominate the thinking that lies behind this discussion. 'F' and 'FAV' begin to work like variables in the physical sciences. They have 'values' and exert 'pulls'. They are to all intents and purposes like vector representations in mechanics. They behave like 'e' and 'm' in physics. A model for this research might be the discovery of Coulomb's Law, which describes the way an electric charge is attracted by other charges. But the issue is that of discrimination – for instance, between people of different race. This is a moral issue and involves such matters as the common moral dilemma between falling in with family loyalties and acting in accordance with the principle to which we, in this society, subscribe: that fairness is an overriding moral good. But FAVs and Fs are the currency of a causal account. So, instead of following through the crises of conscience, the specious accounts offered as justifications for a bit of nepotism, and so on, by which one would get to grips with the workings of a moral order, the author of this passage sets about a laboratory experiment in a meaningless environment, the moral order of which is unknown. A good working criterion for selecting those features of social situations that ought not to be scientized is their relation to moral orders, for then they form part of a very complex network of social and individual rules, conventions, emotions and social expressions of approval and disapproval, real or potential: reference to these is lost in the conditions of experimental work.

Psychology and the natural sciences

Scientism creates a merely rhetorical or figurative connection between the natural and the human sciences, a mere analogy, but there are real relations between biology and various branches of psychology which are complex and subtle. We can look rather briefly and (at this stage) superficially at two cases – the relation between concepts of social action and biological concepts, and the relation between psychological states and processes and those phenomena that are described in neurophysiology.

Social psychology and biology

A basic distinction in the way we would wish to treat the problems of psychology is that between *actions*, the intended movements, cries, etc., by which a creature expresses itself publicly, and *acts*, the social meanings of such actions. Thus a deliberate backwards-and-forwards nodding of the head is an action which, in many cultures, is used to perform the social act of assenting or agreeing. Acts and actions are one of the points at which biology and psychology meet. Different tribes have different repertoires of actions and acts. An important part of psychological research is to discover the origins of these repertoires. Are they biologically derived and genetically maintained (that is, 'biogenic') or are they cultural innovations maintained by imitation and teaching ('sociogenic')? One of the ways of proving that we cannot reduce social psychology to a branch of sociobiology, and yet must allow primate biology a place in human studies, is to examine the possible combinations of biogenic and sociogenic acts and actions. We can find examples of all possible combinations. This is illustrated in the following table.

	Action		*Act*
biogenic	kissing	*biogenic*	expressing affection
biogenic	handshaking	*sociogenic*	betting
sociogenic	displaying coat of arms	*biogenic*	expressing status
sociogenic	signing one's name	*sociogenic*	buying a car

Sometimes we use a form of action to which we seem biologically disposed in order to perform an act that could exist only in a culture. There are also examples of acts that seem to express biologically based human relations for which we use socially and culturally invented actions. Neither the biological repertoire nor the social repertoire is adequate to account for all human social interaction. As our life forms become more complicated, we find new uses for the repertoire of action patterns we have inherited from our biological past. Since this repertoire does not provide distinctive actions to maintain our complex ways of life, however, new devices must be invented and added to the repertoire.

Psychology and neurophysiology

We must find a way to bring not only our general biological inheritance but also our neurophysiology into a proper relation with our psychology. With the help of psychological concepts, and particularly those drawn from the subtle and rich store of ordinary language, we can describe how we process information, how we come to accept or reject certain rules of action, how our emotions are related to our ideas of right and wrong, and so on. The individual components in all these activities and processes are performed by our brains and central nervous systems. To understand this we need to master an important but simple distinction that philosophers of psychology have made between token identity and type identity. By saying that there is an identity between mind and brain we may mean that, whenever a mind-state of a certain type occurs, a brain-state of a certain type occurs. Every time there is a feeling of anxiety, the brain is detecting a flood of adrenalin in the system. If there were thoroughgoing type identity between mind and brain, we could study the workings of the human system in one or the other framework and the results of our studies could be simply translated from one system of concepts directly into the other. Mind talk would be just an alternative way of describing the same thing as we describe with brain talk. But all the most recent work in neuropsychology points to token identity. By that we mean that, although there can never be a mind-state which is not grounded in a brain-state, a certain kind of mind-state is grounded sometimes in a brain-state of one kind, sometimes in another. We cannot then substitute a brain-state description of the workings of human beings for mind-state descriptions because these ways of looking at the system are not systematically correlated. Even though the approach of this book is materialist in general, the fact of token identity means that there must always be a place for an autonomous psychological account of human action and thought.

This is such an important point that we must pause to dwell on it in some detail. It applies both to people in general and to individuals in particular. Suppose we find that a certain neurophysiological area is activated when a certain experimental object, J. Bloggs, recognizes a word or reads a sentence. Donald Broadbent has shown, in the case of reading, that we cannot take for granted that the same neurophysiological mechanisms will be employed by A. N. Other when he or she reads. There may be many ways that 'the brain' can perform the same task, as defined in the concepts of common sense – for instance, reading. Though in a certain sense everyone 'reads with their brain', a neurophysiological description of brain function cannot displace a psychological description of reading. An excellent discussion of this point can be found in Broadbent (1981).

Psychology and common sense

Most schools of 'scientific' psychology make a point of rejecting both commonsense understandings of human psychology and the commonsense categories that go with them and on which they depend. It is sometimes said that they are vague and unreliable. If ordinary language were vague and the judgements made with its help merely subjective, it would be useless for science. Yet if we set aside commonsense psychology in the hope of developing a new and better theory of human thought, action and feeling from scratch, as it were, we must pay a heavy price. The cost is the danger of irrelevance. It is not that scientific psychology must start from commonsense understandings, though that is also true. It is because, for most people and for most purposes, commonsense psychology and its extensions, such as the psychology used in the law, is all that there is. It provides a complete working account of thought and action, and defines the repertoire of our emotions. It represents the 'state of the art', to which scientific psychology may or may not succeed in adding. In practice most people not only use commonsense categories and commonsense ways of understanding for managing their lives and for understanding other people, but also use them as a yardstick for assessing scientific psychology. What can anyone who stands outside the 'profession' make of scientific psychology? There seem to be four relations that can obtain between commonsense knowledge and scientific psychology.

The first is that scientific psychology falls fully within the boundaries of commonsense knowledge, differing from it only in the use of jargon. Once we have decoded it we can see that it amounts to a collection of truisms. Once we learn that the 'risky shift' is the tendency to act more rashly when one is in a group, we can replace it with various well-known adages, such as 'there is safety in numbers' (see Totman (1985) for a very close study of the 'real' content of the alleged 'scientific' conclusions of traditional academic social psychology).

The second possibility is that the results of scientific psychology are quite unconnected with the body of commonsense knowledge and hence largely unusable. For instance, we may read that liking is produced by a decline in response competition and have no inkling how such a finding might be of use in making friends.

The third possibility is that the viewpoint from which the scientific study of behaviour is entered upon is so alien to our moral standpoint that, even if we are willing to accept that there are conditions under which people will act in the ways they are found to, we reject these findings as obnoxious. This is typical of the response of many people to the operant-conditioning principles purportedly discovered by B. F. Skinner. A psychology that reduces human beings to automata is to be rejected as demeaning. If widely believed, it could actually reduce human autonomy by encouraging people to forbear from acting until the appropriate environmental contingency was present.

The last possibility, which comes about rarely either by chance or design, is that systematic, careful, sceptical and rigorous scientific research could be used to extend and correct the domain of commonsense psychology. The pursuit of this kind of programme would permit us to pass beyond the mere making explicit of the principles that are usually tacit in the management of everyday life, largely because they are embodied in practices rather than formulated as explicit rules and adages. On the other hand, if we set off from the firm ground of common sense and started with the exquisitely refined tool of ordinary language, this would eliminate the danger of embarking on a project whose results would have nothing to do with the world as we ordinarily experience it. This last is the standpoint of the approach advocated in this book. For us the task of scientific psychology consists of making the implicit psychologies of everyday life explicit, and then, in the light of that understanding, applying the techniques of *theory-guided* empirical research to develop, refine and extend that body of knowledge and practices.

In short, the answer to the problem of how to relate common sense to scientific psychology is to treat the former as 'part of the literature' – that is, a proper part of the body of knowledge available in the science. It is the platform from which we must start. An excellent example of this approach is the study *Moralities of Everyday Life* by J. Sabini and M. Silver (1982). Each section begins with a detailed analysis of the vocabulary of ordinary language by which the psychological processes to be studied are normally carried on – for example, the identifying of feelings as emotions. Critically interpreted experimental work is brought in to extend and supplement the folk psychology which has been made explicit in the analytical phase of the study. What we believe in everyday life, upon which we base our usual ways of acting – 'commonsense psychology' – would be subject to review and revision if *particular* parts of it gave particular grounds for doubt. For example, it is still a widely accepted principle of commonsense psychology that the more painful a punishment the less likely is someone to repeat the offence for which they received that punishment. This seems not to be true.

The relation of commonsense psychology to scientific psychology is not the same as that between biology and farming, physics and navigation, military arts and architecture, or chemistry and cooking and dyeing. The commonsense component of each of these pairs was an atheoretical *practice*, a set of rules of thumb. The first step to *science* was the development of comprehensive *theories*. But commonsense psychology is itself a theory, or perhaps a cluster of related theories. It recognizes a distinction between obsessional and voluntary action, and builds its explanations of what people say and do around the basic idea of action as the product of agents following rules and conventions to realize their intentions, plans and projects.

The problem with much that is offered as scientific psychology is not that its deliverances are more wrong than right, but that they are not related to anything that we could recognize as a matter of human interest. For example, there are a great many 'results' to be read of experiments concerning intergroup prejudice and bad feeling in which the groups involved had no previous history and no social structure. These 'minimal' groups were supposed to exemplify some sort of 'pure' psychological process that was involved in all kinds of group hostility. It is not just that there are no minimal groups, but that, even if there were, their study would have no clear bearing on the behaviour of people swamped by tradition and led by enthusiasts. The kind of psychology we are advocating in this book would deliberately seek to enhance the understanding people have of one another and to augment their powers of self-management and control. However, such a project must start from the groundwork of the existing psychologies of mankind.

Let us go further. It may not be just that a narrowly conceived version of psychology is less useful than it could be, but it might actually be harmful, morally obnoxious. This could come about in two ways. First of all, there may actually be a lessening of general competence to understand others and to deal with them in a respectful way as a result of the relative impoverishment of the psychological vocabulary. For instance, the term 'helping behaviour', which, as we have pointed out, is adopted by psychologists instead of the ordinary-language expression 'help', is used in such a way that the important moral distinction between 'aid' (help for someone who has some capability but not enough for the job in hand) and 'succour' (help for someone who without that assistance is totally disabled) is glossed over. The conditions under which someone would give aid in a particular culture might be governed by such principles as 'The Lord helps those who help themselves', while succour is thought, at least among those whose moral tales include 'The Good Samaritan', to be required to be given without moral qualification. Second, a scientistic psychology may lead to harmful effects by emphasizing the causes of behaviour to the exclusion of the reasons for action. The more what was traditionally thought to be within the moral sphere is transferred to the causal-technical sphere, the less people are able to act as independent agents; the more they expect to be trained to cope, the more they are inclined to wait passively for the order that relieves them of responsibility. All this comes about when human beings push themselves and others towards certain ideal ways of thinking and even towards certain repertoires of emotions and styles of personality, which they take to be ratified by the studies of psychologists. Some recent studies of autobiography have shown that people make use of a smattering of psychology picked up through the mass media to shy away from taking moral responsibility for their actions.

Finally, we must mention the reciprocal effect of the study of dubious scientistic psychology on the psychologists themselves. For those who stand outside academic psychology, the most marked characteristic of its members is the degree to which they are cynical and alienated from their professional expertise ('It's just a kind of game'; 'We have to do this sort of thing to get grants'; 'We know it's silly or even dishonest but we are forced to go on this way by the profession', etc. etc.), or even debilitated as actors in the ordinary human drama of everyday life. Layfolk frequently comment on the psychological inadequacy of many of those who practise psychology as an academic speciality. If scientific psychology were indeed expanding and critically reviewing the commonsense systems with which we ordinarily work, these comments would be astounding. Their very wide currency does serve to support the view that academic psychology has lost its roots. In our view this is the result of a mistaken effort to emulate an ideal of science based upon a whole series of philosophical errors and historical misunderstandings.

Most scientific psychology exaggerates its own discoveries by undervaluing that with which it competes. It claims that there is no alternative way of understanding people which it must compete with; and compared with nothing it seems to do well. But in a fair comparison it generally does less well than the psychology it purports to displace. Knowledge should not only enable us to repeat those things we already do well, but like a street map it should enable us to find our way about the parts of a terrain we have not explored before. (In this respect the Freudian theory of dreams is an obvious extension of our commonsense and folk beliefs about the source of dream contents.) A street map is of no use if one cannot orient oneself on it by reference to familiar landmarks. Discoveries about the physiological bases of certain emotions are relevant to our emotional lives only in so far as we can relate them to our ordinary experience by means of a shared vocabulary. To take a further analogy: teaching somebody a kind of psychology which systematically fails to connect with their experience is like teaching someone to paint with their eyes shut. After a period of hard training they become better at this curious knack, and the trained shut-eyed painters do much better than mere beginners. All might go on swimmingly, except that someone is bound to come along and point out that it is much better to paint with one's eyes open. By abandoning the skills we ordinarily trust, psychologists often find themselves in the position of the shut-eyed painters, knowing less about personality types, say, than clinical psychologists who have to make assessments of personality every day. The recent surge of criticism from psychiatric social workers against the extrovert/introvert way of classifying personalities is a perfect case in point.

To sum up: scientific psychology is not an infant discipline which will develop into a mature science. It is a combination of false starts involving quite complex intellectual muddles, not the least of which is the tendency to a special jargon we have called 'scientism'. In the succeeding chapters we shall sketch the foundations for a psychology of human thought, action and feeling that may, perhaps, avoid at least some of the errors of the past.

2 WHAT MUST A 'NEW PSYCHOLOGY' BE LIKE?

In this chapter we introduce three main ideas. The conscious control of action relies upon all manner of non-conscious 'sub-routines'. For instance, when one is trying to win a point in an argument one's command of grammar, intonation, and so on, operate automatically in shaping one's speech. Looked at this way, psychology would be a two-tier science, studying conscious control on the one hand and automatic mechanisms on the other. But there is a third level, one aspect of which is the deep structure of the human mind which provides the 'frame' within which conscious action occurs. How-ever, there is another aspect to the third level. Social structures and processes, particularly conversation, impose a second but closely linked kind of framing on our lives. Psychology, we argue, must develop in such a way as to incorporate the study of the third level in both its aspects.

This leads us to the idea of hierarchies. Psychologists need to examine 'constitutive hierarchies' in which the parts of one level be-come the wholes of the next. Syllables are the parts of words, which are the parts of sentences which are the parts of discourses, and so on. But there are also 'regulative hierarchies' in which the choice of highest-level goals determines subordinate goals, right down to the steps to take to bring off some immediate task. So deciding to work for a degree fixes a high-level goal, and that determines many levels of subordinate goals – that one plans to read certain texts, to take certain examinations, and so on. Constitutive hierarchies build 'from the bottom up', while regulative hierarchies build 'from the top down'.

The third idea is the most fundamental of all. It is the idea that thought is first of all a social and collective activity, created in conversation. Individual minds come into existence by 'fencing off' part of the public conversation as a private and individual domain. We shall see how profoundly this idea affects the way a psychological problem field is tackled when we come to describe the new kinds of research opened up by the approach advocated in this book.

Identifying the explanatory domain

Once we have developed a basic analytical method by which we can discover the patterns in human action, a crucial question remains. What kind of underlying processes should we look for in seeking explanations of human conduct? The answer to this question is complicated by the fact that human beings are poised between two 'domains'. Each adult human being has his or her own repertoire of beliefs and habits, the personal domain; but all human action occurs in a social context – sometimes explicit, sometimes implicit – which constitutes the social domain. What anybody does on a particular occasion, therefore, can be fully explained only by reference to both the personal and the social domains. This we call 'the dual control of action'. In the final analysis the sharp distinction between these domains dissolves. Nearly all that is personal to any individual is the result of influences that are predominantly social. The repertoire of emotions a person can feel – even the very organization of conscious-ness itself – comes from the social domain. In Chapter 4 we shall describe some of the ways in which social and collective matters shape personal and individual psychological states and processes. For most practical purposes, however, the psychological study of human action is facilitated by treating the personal and social domains as independent of one another, by regarding both personal intention and social context as contributing to the force of a human action.

In this chapter we concentrate on setting out the general principles of those explanations of human conduct that refer to individual persons only. For any state or process to be explanatory of human conduct it must satisfy certain criteria. It must be a state or process of an individual human being that is sensitive to social context; but to be explanatory it must lie 'behind' conduct, since the state or process is what produces the behaviour. As a psychological explanation it *must* begin with a repertoire of commonsense concepts which refer to mental states and processes. As we have seen earlier, behaviourist or indeed any Humean accounts of human conduct in terms of stimuli cannot meet these criteria and are no more than descriptions of patterns which are yet to be explained. This is true even when the pattern is just an artefact produced by the artificial set-up of an experiment.

Biological psychologies that treat people as neuro-anatomical structures meet one of the above criteria – namely, reference to 'hidden' processes – but do not meet the others. Cognitive and information-processing psychologies that treat people as rational computational devices go some way further towards being genuinely explanatory, but as we will show in greater detail they fail to account for the larger-scale patterns of individual human lives. The setting up of longer-term goals for one's life does not seem to be just a matter of rational calculation. A psychology of the emotions might be just what is needed for us to move closer to a really satisfactory science of mind. Yet psychologists, of all people, seem to have been reluctant to treat human beings as creatures of hope and fear, joy and sadness, pride and guilt. Although, or perhaps because, these things are just what layfolk expect psychologists to deal in, it is just these that we most seldom study.

How might emotion be fitted into an overall theory of psychology, and into what sort of structure would it have to be accommodated? Let us go back to the idea that what is to be discovered must previously have been concealed, and that what is concealed in the natural sciences is usually concealed by factors of scale and pace. It is a property of our sensory system, and most other sensory systems one could imagine, that it does not respond to objects or events which are very small, or very large, or very fast, or very slow. Most of what the natural sciences have discovered, with such spectacular success, has been in just those domains that are hidden from the

senses by reason of scale. Perhaps our ordinary experience of behaviour and of the mind might also be part of a hierarchy of levels
and scales of description, of which only the middle part appears in
our domain of familiar experience. The highest and lowest parts are
hidden from us and remain to be discovered, like microstructures
and macrostructures in the physical world. The domain of physical
nature we experience lies between the hidden realms of atomic
structure on the one hand and the architecture of the galaxy on the
other.

The hierarchies of mind

The hierarchy of behaviour, which has been researched by von
Cranach and others, has the property of most natural hierarchies in
that it is a constitutive structure. The sense in which it is hierarchical
is that small items of behaviour make up larger units of action, which
make up still larger units. It is a hierarchical structure of wholes and
parts. On the other hand, the hierarchy of mental operations – the
control or regulative hierarchy which gives rise to the hierarchical
structure of action – is not primarily a hierarchy of wholes and parts,
but a hierarchy of superordinate controllers regulating the activity of
subordinate controllers. The occurrence of hierarchy in both cases is
a way of managing complexity. As Simon (1981) has pointed out,
all ultra-complex systems in nature are hierarchically structured;
and, if that were not the case, the chances are that they would never
function at all, and we would never be able to understand how they
operated.

In the regulative hierarchy of the mind, the bottom level is made up
of automatic, unmonitored reflex responses. Micro-stimuli, collected by the senses and taken into the system, are collated and
filtered upwards; while, on the output side, hierarchical patterns of
action in displays of motor skill are broken down from global control
units into finer and finer units, until individual nerve impulses make
microscopic contributions to the contraction pattern of individual
muscle fibres. Incoming information is linked to outgoing information at this level, mostly in the form of reflex arcs and other
automatic pre-programmed patterns. There is also feedback control,
in which detailed information about motoric patterns is fed back into
the sensory system to correct and control the pattern of commands to
the motoric system.

It is in this bottom level of the control hierarchy that much of the important work of experimental psychology has taken place. Higher up the control hierarchy, there is a level of information-processing where stimuli have been more richly aggregated and collected into fewer but more complex representations, and at which larger-scale and more complex plans and resolutions to act are formulated. This is where the feed-forward – the anticipation of future action – takes the form of processes we know and monitor consciously, and give names to, such as deciding, planning, reasoning or thinking. The units at this level are perhaps best identified by criteria of meaning-fulness. Words are aggregates of letters. The former are identified as units of meaning; the latter are visually distinguishable physical patterns. It is at this level that what we call the ethogenic method has its place. The term 'ethogenic' was introduced by Harré and Secord (1972) to identify an approach in which the focus of interest becomes the actions for which human beings can be called to account. The method involves the analysis of those accounts in search of the meanings the actors give to their actions and the rules and conven-tions which they follow.

What is at the 'top' of the hierarchy?

At first sight it may seem that this two-level explanation is complete. The mental control system consists merely of the lower-order, fast-running automatic control processes, acting under the guidance of higher-level, conscious, familiar, subjectively monitored pro-cesses. However, bearing in mind the general maxim that most of our perceptions are drawn from the middle range of the hierarchy of things, could it not be that there are one or more higher levels of control process? Perhaps there are levels whose functions are super-ordinate to those of conscious thought, in just the same way that consciousness is superordinate to the control functions of sensory motor reflexes? This is to suggest, in other words, that consciousness is not, after all, the top level of a two-level control hierarchy, but the middle third of a three-level one. This would explain the paradoxical nature of our sense of control over our own affairs. On the one hand we feel we know all the facts that impinge upon us, and we seem to be in control of the actions we perform. We experience ourselves in one sense as being all-knowing and all-controlling. But at the same time life does not go as we want, and we do not understand why. Perhaps our conscious mind is not after all the strategic controller of the system, but just the middle manager of the mind, monitoring and controlling within the limits of its scope, but subject to more compelling and longer-term patterns of authority.

There is a further twist to the story. The top level of the hierarchy, which we would like to suggest is the functional if not the structural location of emotion and motivational processes, is not just another domain in the system waiting to be documented; but it is, in a curious sense, the fundamental part which has always been so illusive. The reason is this: in a constitutive hierarchy of parts and wholes, the properties arise from the bottom upwards. The properties of fundamental particles give their character to atoms, structures of atoms determine the nature of molecules, molecules the cells in a living organism, the cells tissues, and so on. Consequently, in order to analyse such a structure, the important thing is to reduce it to its finest ingredients, because it is from those that the rest of the structure has taken its properties. In so doing, one is tracing the properties of the whole structure back to their origin.

However, with a regulative hierarchy the opposite is the case. Its properties are created from the top downwards. Each of the units and controllers within the overall hierarchy does what it does, and in the way it does, because of the patterns of instructions it receives from above. In that sense, to analyse it is not to start at an arbitrary level and work downwards reductively, but to start at an accessible level and work upwards macro-reductively. It is a matter not of taking things to pieces to see what they are made of, but rather of putting them together to see what they are part of. In the study of behaviour, this situation has proved misleading and has often been misunderstood. Because behaviour is a constitutive hierarchy, it seems that it can be analysed reductively, and the larger units explained in terms of the smaller ones. Somehow the search might lead to the discovery of the behavioural atom. But the behavioural or constitutive hierarchy is a hierarchy only in so far as it is the structured product of a regulative or control hierarchy that takes its properties from the top. Furthermore, there is a correspondence between the two kinds of hierarchy. It is the lower levels in the regulative hierarchy that put the fine detail into the constitutive hierarchy, and it is the higher levels in the regulative hierarchy that contribute the gross strategic pattern to the constitutive hierarchy.

So, although it might seem a paradox to say that in the hierarchy of behaviour the fine details are actually explained by reference to the whole of which they are a part, it is certainly not the case, as so many people have assumed, that the whole can be explained by reduction to its parts. The truth of the matter is that the fine-detailed parts in the behaviour hierarchy are controlled by the lower levels of the regulative hierarchy. But these are accountable to the higher levels of the regulative hierarchy, which make their presence known in the higher levels of the behaviour or constitutive hierarchy. In that sense it is *as if* the fine details of behaviour are explained by reference to the gross structure. And it is therefore in macro-reduction, or upward explanation in the hierarchy, that behavioural analysis is likely to succeed best, rather than in micro-analysis or ordinary 'downward' reduction.

Even in the physical sciences the ultimate question is not what lies at the bottom of the constitutive hierarchy of nature. There is a growing tendency to refer the properties of the fundamental particles to the structure of the universe as a whole. In behavioural science, the correspondingly basic question is what lies at the top of the regulative hierarchy of action. If that top structure is not the conscious mind as we normally experience it, but is some other and more powerful system of regulation lying 'adjacent' to the domain of conscious reasoning, then the most revealing topic domain for psychological enquiry will be found there. This programme of upward explanation, or looking to wholes to explain parts, is applicable only where the hierarchy in question is primarily regulative. So regulation can be both inter- and intrapersonal: it has an individual *and* a social dimension. The relation between individuals and institutions is both regulative and constitutive. Since social and collective patterns cannot be reduced to the level of the individual, this makes the upper level of the individual control hierarchy a joint partner in the determination of the content of conscious experience.

At first sight it might seem strange that the course of evolution has placed a further and more enigmatic level of control on top of that exercised by the conscious mind. It is not that the third level has been 'installed' above the level of conscious control, but rather that, in the course of evolution, and with the gradual increase in complexity of the system as a whole, some but not all of the control process has become conscious. As one would expect, it has been in the penultimate level of the hierarchy that consciousness has proved to be most functional, and has come to be analysed as an information-rich mode of processing and control. This pattern of explanation has become quite common. For example, it is in accord with the work of Galbraith (1977) on the position of the technostructure in industrial systems and the work of Michie (1976) on complex chess-playing artificial intelligence systems, whose information-rich algorithmic control is at a subordinate level to that of a more general heuristic system of pattern-matching rules. This seems to be a fairly common property of complex control systems. It is also found in the legal system, where particular cases are not resolved by a process in which detailed information filters all the way up the system, and then all the way down again in the form of the implementation of rulings; rather, the facts of a case are collected, collated and presented to a court which rules under the guidelines and precedents of higher courts and higher agencies, up to the law-making body of the land.

It seems that the efficient way of running a complex control system is to have a high-level general policy maker, which hands down guidelines to a subordinate information-rich level, at which the facts of particular circumstances are considered in detail, and particular courses of action are chosen. Generalized summaries of the success and failure of different policies filter back up the system, to modify the nature of the high-level policy maker. And that occurs at both 'top' levels of control (see Figure 1). It is our conjecture that the structure of the mind and the social order have evolved along precisely these lines in some kind of co-ordination with the evolution of the structure of language. The information-rich level of decision and control has again ended up in the middle of the hierarchy, where all its richness of visual imagery, representations, knowledge, planning and deliberation go to make up the domain of conscious mentation as we experience it. The crucial task, though, is to find out what are the higher-level strategic processes to which this conscious and familiar level is accountable.

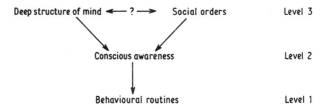

Figure 1   Levels of control hierarchy

Because society is not reducible to an aggregation of individual actions, language and discourse may be a major source of the 'programs' which are assimilated into all levels of this hierarchy to provide it with its 'software structure'.

The ultimate 'units' of mind

If the process is hierarchical as we have suggested, and the top level largely remains to be discovered, then one of the most important features to look for in the analysis of behaviour is its long-term structure. Traditionally, research has been oriented around certain types of behaviour – such as aggression, mating and feeding – and the conditions under which that behaviour is manifested. However, in a control hierarchy different levels of scale do not tend to function as natural units; the overall strategy is at a higher level than the steps needed to achieve its aims. It may well be that one of the most important basic units in the system of behavioural analysis is precisely that which refers to long-term as opposed to short-term patterns, and that this has largely been missed by laboratory analyses. Activities in the laboratory, however naturalistic, can represent only relatively fleeting and fine-detailed patterns of human activity.

Our belief in the existence of real, non-surface social processes arises from the familiar observation that only a blind and misguided atomism would lead us to deny as much reality to the relation between entities as to that of the entities themselves. Marriages are as real as husbands and wives. This suggests that the units of higher levels in the human control hierarchy may be not only greatly extended in time, but also spread over groups of people rather than confined to individuals taken one by one. Marx has familiarized us with the idea that the exigencies of a social system may influence the patterns of our thought and behaviour, regardless of our consciously formulated intentions. But the processes by which such influences come about remain mysterious.

None of this is to deny that there is an important interplay of social and psychological factors, and that each asserts causal powers over the other. Such an interplay implies that concealed and discoverable processes are operating at both ends of the dialogue – for example, the process of psychological symbiosis in which one person provides those mental skills that another, dependent person lacks. The case could be rather like that of a complex computer, which sends 'orders' to some distant sensing and effector devices, and at the same time collects information from them. There is a dialogue between the two, and the computer affects the remote station and is in turn affected by it. The fact that the control apparatus for both parts of the dialogue is predominantly located at the computer's end must not obscure the fact that the sensor is only itself in relation to an extra-systemic reality. For example, a device sensitive to X-rays is defined only for an environment in which there are such things. This model could be applied directly to the psychological symbiosis between a speaking mother and inarticulate infant.

In talking of control hierarchies, it is very easy to assert that one level of control is above another. But how does one know when one process is operating at a higher level than another? There are three criteria according to which a higher-order process may be distinguished from a lower-order one, and according to which social, affective and motivational centres seem to function above those of cognition and conscious decision-making. The first is scope: spatial scope, or the number of body parts that a centre controls; functional scope, or the number of diverse activity types controlled by the centre; and temporal scope, or the duration of any one unit of activity relative to its subordinates. Individual items within the repertoire of moods and emotions appear to be more global than their counterparts in the cognitive or informational repertoire. A mood is longer-lasting than a complaint about the food. The second criterion is many-to-one mapping. There are many units and states in a lower level of control for each one in the higher level of control. Sadness can be manifested in speech, demeanour, posture, and so on. Thirdly, there are two different types of information flow between lower-order and higher-order controllers. Information *per se* flows from the lower-order to the higher-order controller, and its interpretation is governed by the recipient. Commands or instructions proceed from the higher-order to the lower-order controller, and their interpretation is decided by the sender. And it is in that sense that information and command are two different types of message.

The reason for studying this top level of the dual-control hierarchy is that it is, according to this definition, the main controller of action and experience, and in that sense is the real fundamental of the mind, just as DNA or atomic nuclei or tectonic plates are fundamental in their respective disciplines. It is by this level of control that sociobiological and evolutionary imperatives for the gross structure of human action are mediated. It is also to this level of explanation that the laddering of repeated 'why' questions leads in the explanation of actions and mental states in relation to one another. Furthermore, it is the source of many of our practical problems. Except in clear cases of organic damage or psychopathology, few people are practically troubled by the characteristics of their short-term memory or visual system. What they orient to in everyday life, what they feel is worth discussing, and trying to manage, are their hopes and fears, their dreams, anxieties, guilts, worries, and so on, *and* the structural properties of the social relations and institutions in which they find themselves enmeshed. According to this formulation, it is precisely in the highest or third level of control that these things have their origin and their regulation.

Finally, this is the part of the mental apparatus which is most mysterious, partly because one half of it – the social, institutional part – is not individually located at all. It is the part of ourselves which we least understand and which answers the question 'Why do we act as we do?' as opposed to the question 'What is it we do?', which is more familiar and has to do with the second level of the hierarchy, or the question 'How do we do it?', which is generally of less relevance and has to do with the bottom level. This accords with our understanding, and lack of understanding, of our own activity and life patterns. The parts are usually familiar: we know what we experience and what we do. What we do not always know is what are the larger-scale life patterns that these events are part of.

Patterns in the life course

In reviewing the diachronic organization of the life course in ourselves or other people, the primary pattern we notice is the rapidly running fine-detailed pattern, the contingency of response upon stimulus. The relationship between these is the 'primary transfer function', which might be called the behaviour function, and which dictates in the short term which responses will follow from which stimuli. In much human psychology this is represented by culturally specific systems of regulative rules. But that function is not itself invariant. It follows from other higher-order patterns of change and control, and is governed by a second-order function that might be called the 'learning function', which changes the behaviour function in the light of longer-term and more general patterns of experience. This shows up, in practice, in the way rules for acting are culturally specific. The second-order function can itself be conceived as the output of a third-order function, which maps biological and genetic factors to the learning rules, or second-order functions, used by each individual. In practice this third order, or 'epigenetic rule system', in the terminology of Lumsden and Wilson (1981), would have to be studied in relative rather than absolute terms. That is to say, the difference in this function between individuals might be relatable to differences in their genetic endowment, but the absolute nature of the function could not be related to the particular genetic constitution of any one individual. To take a simple case: biological imperatives demand that we eat; but cultural imperatives determine the cuisine, our table manners, and the ritual significance with which many meals are taken.

This hierarchical cascade of acquisition and control would develop primarily downwards, both phylogenetically and onto-genetically – that is, in the development both of a society and of an individual. Primacy would be given to the highest levels, which would be those that were most influenced by early experience. The top-level structures in the control hierarchy are in this view likely to be evolutionarily and developmentally old and simple. And therein lies the danger of our failure to understand and manage them from the more advanced and adult perspective of our second-level conscious monitoring. With the passage of time, a more adult form of the middle level of the mental hierarchy overtakes and overgrows the constantly slow-moving and childlike motivational centres.

The child not only is father to the man but is carried within him as a lifelong pilot whose hand at the controls it is dangerous to neglect. But the adult, rational, cognitive mind has long since lost the characteristics that would have suited it to the operating patterns of the childlike core. The window in the developmental sequence through which the core structures were programmed has opened and closed by the time the individual reaches maturity, leaving in charge a set of global high-level principles which nobody understands at any stage of their development. When the child is a child, the parent does not understand him or her from the perspective of an outsider, and when the child grows up to become an adult, the new and highly specialized patterns of adult conscious reasoning do not easily penetrate the basic rules of the emotional system that were laid down when the cognition was so much younger and so different. Note that this region is not inaccessible as the result of repression, and is quite different from the unconscious as conceived of by Freud.

When two people interact, any level or levels of their three-part hierarchy can be involved. A dialogue between the lowest levels of two people forms a simple sensory-motor exchange in which the motor behaviour of one becomes the sensory information for the other, and vice versa. Table-tennis players or improvising jazz musicians pick up and respond to minute cues from their opponents or fellow musicians, which co-ordinate the parties into a rapidly moving and largely automatic pattern of mutual organization. In a slower or more cerebral case the information is collected over a wider range of cues and a longer period of time, and filtered up through the hierarchy to the level where it forms conscious ideas, concepts, images and conceptions, where it is thought about and compared with memories. Plans are made, verbal formulations considered, and carefully chosen tactics put into effect. This is the interaction of intellects as second-level controllers, much as you would find in the course of an academic seminar, a committee meeting or a conversation. In the conduct of salient, engaging, long-term, close personal relationships, the next stage of the story is seen. Here, patterns of one person's behaviour accumulating in the representation of the other, build up to a level where they can trigger responses in the highest level of control. These responses, filtering down again, are sensed and experienced as affective changes, affection, remorse, regret, hatred, jealousy, love, trust, and so on. They produce far-reaching and long-term shifts in the organization of behavioural planning. These shifts filter further down the system and into the response pattern of that individual. These changes – say, from displays of interest to indifference – have their effect on the first person, filtering up to the third level, and so the cycle proceeds. The interactions themselves form a structure which is locked into the social patterns of the community, and whose overall pattern may be unknown to the participants (see Pearce and Cronen 1980).

The psychological process that drives human relationships is, according to this model, a dialogue of people's emotional systems with the social predicaments in which they find themselves. In the face of both of these we often feel powerless – which might imply that this process is an interplay of the two highest-level, global and long-term controllers in the systems of the two individuals. This could be the reason why interpersonal relationships engage people more deeply than most other activities, and why they have about them an 'existential' quality. They seem to involve and to engage what people are, not merely, in a more concrete and more superficial sense, what they do.

From the standpoint of the conscious actor, which is rooted in the second level of control, the problem is to invent strategies to manipulate and improve one's emotional life and master one's social relations. Since the second level does not exert direct control over the top level, this has to be done by changing patterns of thought and action in such a way that information filtering back up the hierarchy again triggers new emotional responses, which the second level can detect. Since our behaviour towards other people, and their reactions to us, are some of the most powerful triggers to emotional change, it is for the most part by systematic employment of social life that we engineer our emotional life. And it is by putting us in a position where that is our best strategy that our genes govern our conduct in society according to sociobiological imperatives.

There are other strategies too, of course. Acting in relation to situations of opportunity and danger, retreating into fantasy, using alcohol, tobacco and other drugs, all play their part as strategies for the indirect manipulation of the affective centres, the culturally legitimized clusters of emotions and beliefs that form the third level for each human being.

The role of these centres in decision-making is a particularly interesting one. Decision theorists have tried to formulate prescriptive models of optimal decision-making under conditions of uncertainty, in which an individual is seen as trying to maximize a kind of notional score for the success or failure of his or her undertaking. Each possible action has a pay-off if successful, and also a likelihood of success, and the two multiplied together determine the merit of that line of action. As a prescription or redefinition of optimality, that may be fine, but it turns out to be a poor way of describing how people make their selections. It is particularly poor in the case of important decisions. Important decisions, in a multi-level control system of the kind we have been describing, would be taken by a different means. In so far as they were deliberately initiated by the second-level controller or conscious decision-making apparatus at all, they would involve the construction of alternative imaginary futures. A person deliberately constructs systematic and detailed fantasies of possible courses of action and their outcomes. The core process at the heart of the third level of control would react to these imaginings with small emotional shifts and changes, much as it would to these events were they really being carried out. It would be on the basis of this feedback from 'higher authority' that the appeal or lack of appeal of each possible plan would be judged. It goes without saying, of course, that the ground rules of the high-level controller are largely opaque, even to the individual in question, and certainly to other people. For that reason, the more crucial and important the decision, the more paradoxical the outcome. This gives a very pressing practical reason for this kind of psychological processing to be studied, because the effects of other people's salient

decisions on the policies that affect us all are of paramount importance. If, as we suspect, they are governed by the laws of human
irrationality rather than the simpler and more familiar regularities of
rational decision-making, then we had better find out all we can
about them, sooner rather than later. Furthermore, decisions are
rarely made by isolated individuals but 'emerge' in the course of
convention-bounded conversations in highly structured communities.

Evidence for a third level of control

Is this three-level model of the mind nothing more than speculation?
It does seem to fit with a number of lines of argument and evidence
concerning the way the mental system as a whole may be structured.
First, there is its subjective or phenomenological appeal. Life and
experience are lived at mid-scale, and clearly there are events and
patterns both finer-grained and coarser-grained than we normally
monitor. Secondly, it is cybernetically plausible. A complex control
system doing the job the brain has to do would work most adaptively
with this kind of hierarchical division of function. Thirdly, it is
neurologically plausible, since sensory and motor information is sent
to and from the cortex. In humans this has become the seat of a
disproportionately overgrown, second-level, intermediate controller, while in the old centres in the heart of the brain, in the
hippocampus, thalamus and hypothalamus, a more basic animal
form of monitoring takes place, richly interconnected with the cortex
and in mutual interaction with glands and nerve nets all over the
body. Here again, the distinction between a constitutive and a
regulative hierarchy saves us from a possible confusion. We must add
to this the location of every human action in networks of interaction
that spread far beyond the individual actor. In this conjecture, the
affective motivational centres and the structural properties of social
orders are in the highest positions of the dual-regulative hierarchy of
cognitions on the one hand and institutions on the other. That is
quite apart from the constitutive complexity of the former within the
neuro-anatomy of the brain, and of the latter in the child-rearing
practices by which minds are created. There is no contradiction
whatever in the idea that those brain centres which function at the
highest regulative level may be relatively crude and primitive in terms
of their constitutive neurobiological realization, nor that the social
structure may evolve through processes as coarse-grained as Marx's

material dialectic (see Marx and Engels 1973) or Veblen's social emulation (Veblen 1899). (See Harré (1979) for a detailed account of the interplay of these social processes.) Alarming though the idea is, that is precisely what one would expect.

Fourthly, on evolutionary grounds the three-level model again fits with our expectations. Older structures tend to be more autonomous, newer structures more dependent. It is hard to see how an older structure could have evolved which was dependent upon a newer and later one for its functioning. It is not hard to see how a later system could have evolved which is dependent on an earlier or older one. A control hierarchy grows and elaborates downwards. It recruits new elements beneath its existing structure to elaborate it, not on top of the parts that exist already. The only part which is autonomous is the top level. For that reason one would expect that the oldest parts of the brain would be the ones associated with the highest level of regulation, and they are indeed the centres of emotion and motivation, roughly speaking. Just the same temporal relation holds for the relation between minds and social networks. A social order is always prior to the mind of any one of its members.

Similarly, one would expect that the areas of the brain which have most recently grown in proportion and elaborated their contribution to the overall mechanism would be the ones that are comparatively lower in the overall system of regulation. In brains, as in countries, the head of state remains the same size and the bureaucracy gets bigger and bigger.

Finally, it may be that this three-level view is also consistent with our cultural experiences of art, music and religion. Lodged as we are as intellectual beings beneath the controlling umbrella of a phylogenetically old system of biological drives and feelings and embedded in networks of social relations that ramify beyond our limited visions, we view our world as one in which forces more powerful than ourselves are the bringers of distress or comfort. Authorities higher than our own are responsible for our destiny, and artefacts that give us a feeling of pleasure or sadness move us in a way which seems more fundamental than the facts and figures of referential discourse.

What, then, is this high-level control system like? If its external relations are as we have suggested, what is the nature of its internal relations, its parts and processes? As yet there is not much to be said. It is by definition a control device whose two main 'modules' are, at first sight, of radically different kinds. On the one hand, there is a piece of the brain's cybernetic machinery which maps features of our cognition, our streams of consciousness, to changes in our affective state. On the other hand, there are the seething networks of social relations in which we are embedded; the rules or patterns or data structures by which these interact and jointly influence us are what we wish to find out. The regularities they produce are not simple, and probably far from universal. How much simpler it would be if each emotion had its trigger, one and only one location in a universal system of morality, and responded in proportion – if danger produced fear and opportunity produced hope, if success produced pride and failure disappointment. But for many people fear is out of all proportion to danger even as they perceive it, and the greatest hope often springs from the least likelihood of success. There is an elusive pattern to emotional life which structures everything we do, but it is not in itself the simple system of pushes and pulls that it might seem at first sight. What is responded to – the triggers in an individual – may be complex and abstract. They may be life themes like success or poverty, control, death, freedom, responsibility or parenthood. The recent work of Schank (1982) has suggested that memory can be triggered by such abstract configurations of events as asking repeatedly for more and more of something and never getting enough. An abstract level of similarity is sufficient. Jean-Pierre de Waele has demonstrated the same point, in that the problem and conflict situations he uses to enhance recall of life events are reproductions only of the logical or abstract properties of those events – such as the successful use of a strategy followed by a failure. Requests for a shorter and shorter haircut trigger spontaneously the memory of a time when rarer and rarer steaks were wanted but never came. In the higher and still more abstract levels of emotional schematization, the triggers for each affect, and the patterns of reaction they can give rise to, may be very far from our simple expectations. Maybe the emotional schemata are, after all, not unlike the archetypes of the collective unconscious.

The control hierarchy does not just exist in the here-and-now. For any one level of control, there are higher-order programs by which its programs are collected and inserted. Even a simple model of the overall systems would have to allow for four types of processors: a cognitive controller which maps circumstances to actions; an affective controller, operating at a higher level, which changes the circumstance–action mapping that is currently in force; a cognitive learning routine which builds up the library of circumstance–action rules that can be called upon; and an affective learning routine which builds up the repertoire of reactions and rules by which changing circumstances are mapped to emotions and moods, and thence to alterations in the circumstance–action pattern.

In principle these speculations can be connected to empirical methods of research. The primary manifestation of the high-level control or core process in the human individual, as we have suggested it, would be the nature of the relationships between circumstances and moods and emotions. This would appear as a 'black box' in the mind, a mysterious mechanism with a detectable input–output regularity, at least in the empirical domain of the individual's consciousness. Reports of how circumstances and emotions are related would be treated with reserve. The problem of what is in the 'black box' could be addressed in much the way that Powers (1973) suggests in his hierarchical model of the mind. We could follow his procedure for determining the control rules. One would propose candidate rules and make systematic changes in the input, together with predictions about what the output change should be, until a disconfirmation appears and the rules have to be revised – the method we have described in detail for 'second-level' research. Secondly, the unique role of the high-level controllers is to control the long-term behaviour patterns of the individual. In this respect, psycho-biographical work such as that of Jean-Pierre de Waele should give many of the clues to the organization of the core structure. (See de Waele and Harré 1977, 1979.) It is in so far as the life course of individuals is more regular, and organized over a longer term than they are aware of contriving deliberately, controlled in part by the social patterns and moral orders within which they live, that evidence for third-level control will be found. The long-term patterns such as those Goffman has called 'moral careers' could be there because the social environment is highly organized and provides for piecemeal reactions which eventually produce longer-term patterns than one is aware of producing deliberately.

A theory of this kind can also be tested by modelling, either using artificial analogues such as AI programmes, or by using Woods's method of human partial simulations (Woods 1970), in which groups of people carry out collectively a task that would normally be assigned to an individual, with their respective roles and channels of communication designed to reproduce alternative conceptions of mental organization. The relative realism and other characteristics of their performance in different organizations could be taken as evidence for the acceptability of each arrangement as a simulation of the real control structure.

There must be stringent empirical tests before such hypotheses as these are accepted, and we should not be too lenient with conjectures that have not yet been tried and tested. But if we are too sceptical about theories and evidence, as some people have been in psychology, then the result will be that false positive assertions about what could be the case are avoided only at the expense of large numbers of false negatives – assertions as to what is not the case. It could be that we have set up the subject with a conception of scientific rigour and accuracy which absolutely and permanently precludes our finding most of what is true and worthwhile in human understanding. It could also be argued that truth and falsity are not the only discriminands of good and bad scientific ideas. Some of the true ideas may be much better than others in their novelty, coherence, generativity, utility, and so on; similarly, some of the false ideas may be much more useful than others. If our methodology is addressed solely to the dichotomizing of the world of propositions into a pile called 'true', each of which is subsequently given equal reverence, and a pile called 'false', each of which is subsequently viewed with equal disdain, then much of what is valuable will be lost, and much of what is banal and trivial will be worshipped undeservedly in the temple of truth.

As yet all of this is mostly speculative – a conjecture awaiting refutation, as Popper would have it; but, before refutation can succeed or fail, the ideas themselves must be taken seriously and tested seriously.

The idea of 'cognitive science'

Psychology, like other forms of human enquiry, is littered with good old words which have been put to new uses. An unfortunate example is the word 'model'. It is now used by psychologists, though by no other academic group, to mean what the rest of the learned world means by 'theory'. Its original dual meanings of 'analogue' and 'ideal' have been lost. Another, much more important word, has lately shifted in sense. This is the term 'cognitive'. In its original acceptation it meant 'pertaining to thought'. After virtual banishment from the lips and pens of psychologists during the heyday of behaviourism it has now reappeared in such phrases as 'cognitive science'. In this new use it means 'pertaining to information-processing'. Since some of the advocates of the new approach believe that thinking *is* information-processing, it is easy to see how this shift in usage came about. 'Cognitive' is now used to describe a special kind of psychological theory in which an explanatory model (in the old sense of 'model') of the process involved in some human activity – such as remembering, classifying or perceiving – is developed. By a somewhat complex series of analogies the hypothetical processes represented by the model are conceived as kinds of 'information-processing'. The analogies are complex since neither 'information' nor 'processing' is used in its usual way in this context.

In our view this is a development generally to be welcomed. In this book we shall follow the new usage of the term cognitive, though we would wish to repudiate two of its implications. We do not believe that thinking *is* information-processing, though some forms of thinking can usefully be compared to it. The other implication is the individualism with which contemporary cognitive science is infected. We can see no evidence for the widespread supposition that 'information-processing systems' are exclusively to be identified with structural properties and modular analyses of individual human beings. In many cases psychologists will find it more fruitful to treat some social group as an information-processor, each member of the group having a specific function as a 'module' within the total system. Conversation can provide the channels of information flow. With respect to the distinctions drawn in this chapter, 'cognitive science' is a technique for imagining hypothetical mechanisms that operate at the lowest tier of our three-tier science.

3 HOW DOES AN EXPLANATORY SCIENCE WORK?

In the last chapter we described the task of an enriched psychology in terms of three main ideas. The first was that the management of human action involves three levels of control, two of which – the conscious control of action in the following of rules, and the system of higher order constraints of which, as individuals, we are barely aware – have hardly been seriously studied. The second was the idea of two hierarchies: a regulative hierarchy by which action is controlled, and a constitutive hierarchy by which units are assembled into higher order structures. The third idea was that social and collective processes, particularly those which are carried on through conversation, are the main determinants of the form of human minds.

These three ideas open up the possibility of many new kinds of studies, and new domains of enquiry. In order to pursue them, though, we need to have a clear idea about how an explanatory science is built up. In this chapter we show how this is achieved in the physical and biological sciences by the use of structures of analogies. One of the most important kinds of explanatory theory is involved in structural explanations and we explain, in detail, how structural explanation is achieved.

Recent studies in the history and philosophy of science have revealed much more clearly than before how the conceptual foundation of a science originates and grows. One thing is perfectly clear – there is no such thing as a pure or concept-free 'fact'. Data arise as the result of an interaction between a growing conceptual system and a partially revealed and changing world. Of the various ways in which concepts arise prior to the facts or data they enable us to create, the use of analogies is among the most important. We explain how 'analytical analogies' can be applied to vaguely defined phenomena of interest to bring out certain aspects for study. In much the same way a cytologist might stain a bacterium to reveal some of its internal architecture. What he or she sees will be partly determined by the particular stain chosen.

The 'analytical' use of analogy is complemented by the role of source analogies in controlling the way theoretical concepts are invented to describe the unobservable processes that are thought to produce the patterns we can pick out with our analytical analogies. Because much of what we pick out in the study of thought and action is structured or patterned, a particular kind of explanation – structural explanation – is emphasized in this chapter. In the first chapter we explained why the other main kind of explanatory format, the cause–effect explanation, is of lesser importance in psychology.

The everyday world, from the study of which the physical sciences developed, is poised between a micro-world of molecules, atoms, electrons, quarks, and the like, and a macro-world of solar systems, gravitational and electromagnetic fields, galactic formations, and so on. The observable physical properties of ordinary things are the joint result of their microstructure and of their location in the macrostructure. The mass of a material body is the sum of the mass of its parts, but the mass of any body is now believed by physicists to be ultimately explicable by reference to the universe as a whole. Biology similarly recognizes the organism as a being poised between its anatomy and its ecology. To complete our account of explanatory science, we introduce the distinction between microstructural and macrostructural explanations, both of which will be needed in a truly scientific psychology.

The nature of theories

Analytical models

We have already noticed the essential role of concepts in eliciting facts. Where do such concepts come from? One way of understanding both the origin and the use of concepts in the creation of facts is to see the process in terms of an analogy, which we will call the 'analytical analogy'. First of all, an example from the physical sciences: the law 'pressure × volume = a constant' was discovered by the use of an analytical analogy. Robert Boyle was interested in the problem of the vacuum. Why were there no naturally occurring vacua in the ordinary world? Was it because of a divine prohibition, or was it the effect of a natural process? If air was elastic (springy), it would tend to expand to fill the empty places as they came to be formed. Boyle's research was controlled by an analogy. Load a spring of metal with a weight and it is compressed. We can study the properties of the spring by measuring the amount of that compression caused by different weights. Boyle made a spring of air. He compressed the air by filling the open arm with mercury, and used the analogy with a metal spring to construct (elicit) a series of observations from which he inferred his famous law. The spring was an analytical model.

Now let us apply this idea in psychology, with a simple example. When one watches the behaviour of people in public it is by no means always obvious what they are doing, nor how to describe it. One must have some scheme for analysing their behaviour. One may need different schemes for groups of differing size. Where do such schemes come from? If we are to follow the lead of the physical sciences, we must call up one or more analytical analogies. Is there something familiar with which the behaviour or structure or discourse of the group of interest is analogous? The great merit of the work of Erving Goffman has been the skill with which he chose and applied fruitful analytical analogues (see Goffman 1969). The simplest, and one of the most powerful, was the comparison of many activities of everyday life to theatrical performances. If a doctor's surgery is compared to a stage setting, and the doctors, their staff and patients to the players, all sorts of interesting patterns of behaviour emerge from the immensely complicated flow of events that occur during routine consultations. We shall develop this analytical analogy further in our exposition of the techniques Marsh used in his studies of football hooliganism.

Shrewd choice of an analytical analogue is the beginning of the discovery of structure. Science begins with what we could call 'common experience'. We add to that an analytical model, and so we elicit a pattern that would have been invisible without the model.

We must be careful, however, not to confuse analysis with explanation. The power of an analogy to reveal structures in the flow of events does not entitle us to assume that the 'mechanisms' by which the events are produced in the analogue are the same as those by which the corresponding events are produced in the kind of episode we are studying. To say that some of the steps to building a friendship are like rituals does not imply that the ways in which those steps are managed are like the ways in which rituals are performed. They may or may not be. In general it is not possible to discover the mechanisms or processes whereby patterns are produced by using the same kind of observations or experiments through which the pattern itself was revealed. These points can be made clear with another example from the natural sciences.

Source models

A very simple and clear example of how explanations come into being is Darwin's theory of the origin of species. It is probably still impossible to observe the process of organic evolution, and it was certainly out of the question in Darwin's day. It is too slow and on too large a scale. Darwin's discovery of the mechanism of evolution was made not by observation but by thought. In *The Origin of Species* (Darwin 1859) he describes exactly how he proceeded and encourages readers to make the discovery for themselves. Darwin begins by describing how domestic variation – variation between generations of animals and plants in a farm or garden – can be used to create domestic novelties, new kinds of plants and new kinds of animals. The process is genetic selection. He describes how a gardener looks over his plants and throws away the seeds of those from which he does *not* wish to breed the next generation. The theory of organic evolution is created by using the phenomenon of domestic selection as a source model, an analogy. There is known to be natural variation; there is known to be natural novelty – that is, new species appear in the fossil record. But what is the process by which the new species are created on the basis of natural variation? By the end of the book's second chapter we are forced to the same conclusion as Darwin.

The pattern of reasoning runs as follows:

Domestic novelties (new breeds) are created by domestic selection from domestic variation
Natural novelties (new species) are created by (what?) from natural variation.

Everybody who follows the argument thus far must say 'natural selection'! The analogy with the source model allows us to complete the theory. However, it is very important to remember that the relation between domestic and natural selection *is* an analogy. Darwin discusses its limits by pointing out which features of domestic selection can be transferred to natural selection and which cannot. For example, in domestic selection there is a person who intends to select. There is no apparent intention in natural selection. When we choose a source model and use it to create a theoretical explanation, we must be very careful to examine the central analogical relation to see what can legitimately be transferred from source to theory and what cannot.

Use of both models

What of the status of the various components of our science? The pattern we have discovered using an analytical model is real, though it is a limited selection from all possible available patterns. But the behaviour of the explanatory mechanism which is created by use of the source model is imaginary. It has not been observed; it has been thought. Our analytical model reveals a behaviour pattern, whatever the real mechanism that produces it. The first assessment of a theory is internal. We must ask whether the source model creates a conception of a productive mechanism which could be real. The imagined mechanism or process must be of the right kind for the place in nature it is supposed to occupy. But it must also work well: it must simulate the behaviour of the real process convincingly. Darwin imagined how natural selection would work to produce changes in the bodily forms and behaviour of animals and plants. He found they were like the real patterns he had discovered by observation, and this we can call the analogy of behaviour. But the real pattern was caused by a real process. What is the relation between our hypothetical or imagined process and the real process? To answer this we need to take our discussion of how the natural sciences work a stage further. We shall discuss the development of test procedures for imagined causal processes in a later section. To create a truly scientific psychology we should try to construct psychological explanations in the same way as explanations are built up in the natural sciences, particularly in biology.

An example will help to clarify the application of analytical and source models to a psychological problem field: the work by Peter Marsh (1978) on violence at football grounds. Strange things happen at a British football ground – scarves are waved, songs are chanted, and so on, but strangest of all are groups of young men threatening and abusing each other and occasionally coming to blows. The first step to a scientific treatment of these events is to see these matters as enigmatic. We do not understand, in the sense that we do not have an adequate way of describing what is happening. We need an analytical model. The basic analytical model used by Marsh was that of a drama, a staged play. The enigmatic events are regarded as if they were performances by actors in costume, on a stage, playing for an audience. Using the idea of a stage play, Marsh could look for certain kinds of patterns in the behaviour and dress of the people involved. But this analogue or model does not explain how the typical behaviour patterns of 'aggro' were produced. Clearly football hooligans are *not* actors imitating the behaviour of football hooligans. Another model – a source model – is required to provide us with an analogue for the unknown process by which 'aggro' is produced. An important contribution is the idea that a fruitful source analogue for much human action can be found in the way conscious agents deliberately follow explicit rules. The problem of how to explain 'aggro' performances then becomes well defined: are there rules or rule-like beliefs – that is, beliefs about what should or should not be done, implicit and/or explicit – that were being followed? And how did hooligans come to know them?

Compare the programme of Marsh's investigation with one based on a different analogue. In the work of Desmond Morris (1983), a different source model was used to formulate an explanation of the same patterns of violent behaviour. He used an ethological model, based upon treating football fans *as if* they were just male animals. Morris looks for an explanation of hooliganism in terms of a biological process of sexual selection, ultimately driven by a certain genetic endowment. This set of genes has evolved through the process by which male animals form a status hierarchy. The test procedure for seeing whether that conception pictures the causal mechanism actually operative in the real world would be different from the test procedure for looking for systems of rules. This example shows how important it is to identify clearly the often tacit source model with which one is constructing one's theory.

In a perfect theory the analytical analogue and the source analogue are co-ordinate: they draw on the same basic material. In ethogenic psychology we use an analytical model which is a development of the analogy of the stage play, and this is strongly co-ordinate with the image of an actor following a script as source model. It is less strongly but still adequately co-ordinate with the image of a player of a game following a rule. But in real life, in many cases, people are not aware of following rules, yet their actions are smoothly patterned. So, like Darwin, who explored the similarities and differences between domestic selection and natural selection, we must explore the differences between rules in the literal sense and the use of a metaphorical notion of 'rules' to describe a hypothetical 'something' that is normative, cultural and propositional, and active in the control and management of action. (We shall return to that point in discussing structural explanation.) This, then, is the kind of technique we need for thinking scientifically in a sophisticated way.

In the positivistic distortion of science, too long an influence in psychology, only one part of this structure appears. Only the pattern of observed behaviour and its generalized description appear; all the rest is missing. But in the theoretical work of natural scientists – in biology, in physics, in chemistry, in physiology, in cosmology – the whole structure is used, though much of it is tacit. If we are to make psychology properly scientific, we must make use of a more sophisticated conception of science than the simple structure picked out by the positivist theory of science. As we will show, this practical guide to research meshes very nicely with recent developments in cognitive science.

To summarize, we need an analytical model acting on common experience to pick out observed patterns. These are real patterns, so must be produced by a real mechanism. In the initial stages it is not observable, so is problematically related to a temporary but research-guiding 'stand-in'. This is the imaginary process thought out on the basis of an analogy to a source model or analogue. The elements of this scheme need not be in the head of any one person. The totality of required components might be realized only in a community of scientists, a research team. Someone develops the analytical analogue, someone else the source analogue, and so on.

Some recent work on the theory of analogy can be used to enlarge our understanding of the kinds of judgements of similarity and difference typical of analogical reasoning. There is a useful distinction to be made between the positive, negative and neutral aspects of analogy. The positive analogy comprises the similarities between subject and analogue, the negative the dissimilarities, and the neutral comprises those aspects of both that have not yet been compared.

The relation between real and imaginary processes

Characteristically in science, theoretical terms get their meaning through the analogies of the processes they describe to the source models upon which the theory is finally based. The theoretical concept 'rule-following' describes something that is an analogue of that which the literal concept 'following a rule' describes. The latter might be used to refer to the way new members of a committee consciously consult and follow standing orders regulating the way business is to be conducted. Experienced legislators rarely consult the written rules. When we describe them as 'rule-following' we imply that the non-conscious process by which their behaviour is regulated has certain similarities to conscious rule-following. But analogues are both similar to and different from their sources. The similarities define our procedures for searching for the real processes and mechanisms described in theory, while the differences warn us that we cannot expect them to be exactly like those with which we are familiar.

The use of terms like 'rule' in source analogues and the associated theory raises a fundamental problem for psychological science. In their literal use in the source analogue, such terms are clearly mentalistic. Rules belong in the same world as items of knowledge and beliefs. But when we use the term 'rule' in the new theoretical context, as simile or perhaps metaphor, does it still refer to something of the same general sort? To find a rule in the literal sense, we look for a normative belief realized in an inscription or spoken convention. To find a 'rule' in the analogical or figurative sense perhaps we should look for a typical pattern of neural events, a certain molecular organization of the chemistry of brain cells, or something of that sort?

Do the terms in which they build theories in what is now called 'cognitive psychology' really refer obliquely to physiological processes and states of the brain, or is there a realm of hidden (non-conscious) psychological states and processes which cognitive theories help us to uncover, in the way atomic and molecular theories in chemistry help us to uncover the hidden structures of wood, coal, water, and so on?

The vocabulary of psychology grows precisely by extending the network of *psychological* concepts to construct *as it were* a series of events described in terms appropriate to conscious mental activity, complementary to the unconscious processes by which actions are generated. The question 'Are there unconscious mental processes?', looked at one way, must be answered in the affirmative, since we have no alternative but to develop a way of speaking in which whatever it is that intervenes in the gaps of the 'broken chain of conscious events', as Freud called it, is described in the same terms as that chain, and necessarily so, since it is in those terms that the very gaps to be filled are defined. Taken another way, the question must take the answer 'No! There are no such processes.' All that could intervene between one conscious state and another is a physiological process, for which these psychological concepts provide an alternative description.

The concepts of ethogenic psychology as a cognitive science of social action are constructed on just this basis. Conscious experience is ordered in such a way that psychological concepts like 'rule', 'plan', 'project', etc., are called into being to fill the gaps in our account of that order. Much social life is carried on without conscious attention to the means by which intended acts are achieved. So, to the question 'Are there subjective rules?', the answer must be: 'Of course, since that is how I have chosen to speak of the underlying processes that generate our conduct.' But taken another way the answer is firmly 'No'. All that is being referred to in the realm of nature, so to speak, is a hierarchical process of reflexive modelling within a physiological device. But the workings of this device must be *described* in mentalistic terms, since the products of its activities appear to us through manifestations in conscious experience, as plans, intentions, emotions, and so on.

In the last analysis, the practice of developing theoretical concepts by analogy from and metaphorical transformation of established concepts, though conservative, and sometimes paralysingly so, secures the intelligibility and, in principle, the testability of theory. The analogy relations fix at least some part of the 'deep grammatical' rules for the concepts in use in the corresponding theory. This constraint makes it possible to formulate specific existential questions, since attention to some of the rules for using the concepts of the source model allows scientists to know where to look for an instance of the sort of entity or process they have hypothesized.

Structural explanation

Template and product

Many of the sequences of events we can observe by using an analytical model are structures – groups of standard elements or 'parts' in fixed relations. For example, a quarrel may develop between two people who are closely related always in the same fixed way, and proceed step by step to an identical resolution each time it breaks out. The basic idea of the structural approach can be expressed in a principle of structural explanation: if there is a structured product, there will be something else with a similar structure somewhere in the conditions that produced that product. So, knowing the structure of some psychological episode – for example, the steps in an individual person's reasoning out the solution to a problem, or the sequence of moves made by a group of people playing a game, etc. – we look for a structural similarity between the observed structure and some organized feature of the conditions that engendered it. Let us call the structure to be found among the conditions a 'template'. The product and the template must match each other if we are to be able to use the structure of the template to explain the structure of the product. There must also be reason to believe there is a process of replication by which the template is actually involved in the creation of the product.

There are different kinds of structural explanations all obeying the general principle 'Templates shape products'. We can use this idea to define one of the tasks for psychological explanation: find the template responsible for the pattern or structure of some social event. There are very simple examples where we have no difficulty at all in discovering the template. Week by week mass is celebrated by the Catholic Church all over the world, in ceremonies which have essentially the same structure – that is, the same parts are performed in the same order. Though the languages are nowadays different, the sequence of acts – that is, meaningful actions – is the same: the elevation of the Host, the blessing, and so on, are repeated hundreds, thousands, perhaps millions of times a week. How is this similarity to be accounted for? It is easily explained by the existence of a template which shapes each individual performance. There is a book of rules which priests follow the world over to create the mass. The rules specify items, and the order of their performance must be followed for a mass to have been performed. The mass is a very simple case, since there is only one kind of rule controlling the event. But in a game of football the relation between the rules and the game is much more complicated. There are constitutive rules, such as the require-ment that each side must have eleven players. But there are also strategic and tactical rules controlling play, while leaving open the exact way in which they are realized. This means that each game can be different in certain respects.

In using the idea of rule-following to explain social events, an analogy with football and other games can be very useful. But there are some social and psychological events which are more like the mass, in which the structure is produced very exactly, time after time. There has been a good deal of study of the way people are introduced to each other in different cultures. There are definite and precise structures in each distinctive culture for making introductions. In English introductions there are five distinct stages, but there should be no mention of the profession or social status of the people being introduced. That has to be discovered or disclosed in an informal interaction at the end of the ceremonial part of the introduction. Other cultures order informal ceremonies differently. In Denmark the introduction ceremony includes the exchange of information about the profession and social status of the people being introduced. The principle of structural explanation defines various research problems. What is the cognitive status of the template that deter-mines the very strict creation and re-creation of structure in each culture? Is it perhaps habit, or informal rule? And in what develop-mental process is that template learned? These are quite difficult problems, because the 'rules' of informal social interaction are mainly tacit. By the time they are explicitly formulated in etiquette books they are usually a few years out of date.

Three kinds of structural explanation

So far we have given only a very general description of structural explanation. More detailed study reveals three different ways by which structures are produced. The first kind we could call 'assemb-lage' – the fitting together of parts. In assemblage there is often no pre-existing template of the whole product. The parts of the structure are such that they can fit together in only one way. This kind of structural explanation is very rare in the social sciences, but it is common in the physical sciences. A very good example is the way in which the structure of a diamond is created. A diamond is an assemblage of carbon atoms, each carbon atom having a tetrahedral structure. When they go together to form a diamond they can fit together in only one way. There is no overall plan for a diamond, but all diamonds have the same crystalline structure because they are all made of the same kind of structured parts.

The second way in which structure is produced is 'reproduction'. In reproduction the product and the template both exist separately. The template can be used many times to create many examples of the product. Each priest has one book but he can use it to control the performance of hundreds and hundreds of masses. In reproduction, rules often form the template. The most important feature of a reproduction process offered in explanation of an observed pattern is that the structure of the template continues to exist after the product has been created.

There is a third kind of structure creation which we could call 'transformation'. In transformation the template becomes part of the product. For example, in Lévi-Strauss's structural theory of myth (Lévi-Strauss 1968), myths are created by absorbing the structure of a previous myth into a new myth. A myth is created by a process of transformation, not reproduction. In many cases of social analysis we need to think in terms of transformation. For example, in studying the way in which a football game develops, one must look for the pattern of interaction between the players which continually develops but retains a basic structure reflecting the manager's strategic and tactical plans.

Microstructure and macrostructure

In Chapter 2 we brought to the fore the importance of the insight that, in trying to explain human thinking and acting, feeling and striving, we need to pay attention both to 'parts' of individual human beings and to larger wholes, such as families, of which these individuals are themselves 'parts'. Structure plays an important role in both kinds of explanation.

Why is an assemblage of parts able to do things that none of the parts can do separately? Why can a tractor climb a hill but a gear wheel or a rubber tyre cannot? The answer is simple but of profound significance. The special power of the tractor – that is, of the whole –

comes about because of the way the parts have been put together. This is also true of the things put together by nature. A piece of gold has different properties and powers from a mere rabble of millions of protons, neutrons and electrons. These properties emerge when the sub-atomic particles take up a certain configuration, the protons and neutrons forming the nuclei and the electrons arranged in stable orbital shells. Micro-explanation involves not only a catalogue of the relevant components but an account of the way the parts are organized as a structure.

Both the physical and the social sciences have long recognized that many of the properties and powers of material and of social beings come into existence because the being concerned is related to some larger structure. A judge has certain powers that are not possessed by an ordinary citizen because as a judge he or she is occupying a role position in a legal system. Such a system is a macrostructure. In physics the inertia of a material body (its power to resist the accelerating effect of a force) is nowadays thought to be due not to some intrinsic property of the body but to its relation to all the other bodies in the universe. Here the notion of structure is more tenuous. These are macrostructural explanations. We shall suggest that psychology too can fruitfully look for both kinds of explanation, often the one complementing the other. In Chapter 7 we show how a complementary use of both kinds of explanation leads to considerable advances in the study of the emotions.

4 WHY IS COGNITIVE PSYCHOLOGY NOT ENOUGH?

The basic idea behind cognitive psychology is that for each mental function, say remembering, there is a mental 'module' which performs that function (Fodor 1983). This idea is an important advance but it cannot lead to a complete psychology, for several reasons. In this chapter we show how many mental functions involve not only individual processing of information but also certain social processes involving the participation and interaction of more than one individual. Furthermore there are important branches of psychology in which the mental activities required to perform a certain class of activities, such as greeting strangers, can be explained by reference to the same processing modules which are supposedly at work in some quite different kind of activity, such as choosing a brand in a supermarket.

All this can be neatly described by the use of the product–process distinction. Since, from the point of view of the commonsense criteria by which we pick out distinctive human activities, greeting strangers and selecting brands are distinctive products of some mental activity, the supposition that they are created by the working of the same process upsets any simplistic programme of reading off the modules from the functions, as these are defined in commonsense terms. But cognitive psychology, as it is currently practised, locates the processing modules in the minds/brains of human individuals. The task of explaining what people do cannot be completed even when we take the step of using the 'many product/common process' principle because of the involvement of a social dimension in the explanation of human action. To support this important development we show in detail where 'collectivist' considerations must be included. Four domains are defined: public-collective, private-collective, private-individual and public-individual, in each of which there are characteristic psychological products and processes. We show, in outline, how features of public-collective activities, particularly conversations, must be taken into account in understanding how individual persons think, feel and act. Finally we introduce the idea of psychological symbiosis, the process by which people supplement each other's psychological capabilities and resources to maintain the level of mental functioning deemed appropriate for the group to which they belong.

The modularity hypothesis

The main principle of cognitive psychology is that many important psychological functions, like recognizing an object as belonging to a certain kind, are to be treated as the work of independent information-processing modules. These modules can be thought of as 'organs', on the model of the organs of the physical body which are identified by function as well as by form. The kidneys are the organs which 'do' filtering. The language organ, if there were one, would be the organ which 'did' syntax. Modularity analysis is the intermediate step between the study of human performances in their own terms (the task of ethogenic psychology) and both neurophysiology and microsociology. In neurophysiology we attempt to identify and investigate the neural processes and structures which are the 'hardware', the physical basis of information-processing modules. In microsociology we study the social-relational structures and processes of exchange by which groups of people process information, in their conversations and other symbolic interactions. Few branches of psychology map neatly on to only one kind of plausible modular hypothesis. For instance, in the study of memory, though each person has a 'memory module' we must also take into account the social processes by which individual recollections are certified as bona fide memories.

Some alleged modules are currently in dispute. A number of very complicated issues confront the attempt to define and prove the existence of a 'language organ'. But social action, while susceptible of ethogenic treatment to pick out its parts and structures, does not seem to call for the hypothesis of a 'social action information-processing module' or 'sociality organ' to be located in individual social actors. Social action involves means–end reasoning, some-times done individually but more often collectively; but then so does fixing cars. Social action involves the categorization of physical entities such as facial expressions, gestures, etc., by reference not just to their physical properties but also to their meanings; but so does reading. And so on. What descriptive psychology sees as different *products* may be generated by the operation of the same underlying mechanisms – by the working of similar *processes*, operating upon different materials. It follows that, while (from the point of view of common sense) social action is a phenomenon distinctive from day-dreaming, both may depend on the same set of information-processing modules, so far as the individuals involved are concerned.

Thus, according to the realist or anti-positivist account of science, a scientific study of thought and action must be directed to discover-ing the processes that produce those phenomena. Behaviour *per se*, whether social or otherwise, is only a surface phenomenon, a part of ordinary common experience, and the real questions it poses do not concern its nature so much as its origins. On the whole we are puzzled not so much about what human social behaviour, or human emotional experience and display, is like, as about *why* it is that way. Social psychology must therefore do more than merely identify the characteristics of social behaviour as such, or of the psychology of the emotions and expressive displays. Likewise the natural sciences, which appear to deal with the behaviour of particular materials, their physical structures, and so on, are seldom content just to catalogue their overt properties. They are much more concerned, in the main, to discover from which underlying constituents or features these properties come. The science of chemistry is devoted to linking observed chemical properties to hypothetical atomic structures. Observable behaviour is often the test of a theory, but what the theory attempts to describe is the origin of that behaviour, rather than the behaviour itself. Taken literally, the idea of a science of behaviour in general, or of social or linguistic or any other kind of behaviour in particular, is very unscientific. As Noam Chomsky put it: 'As a general designation for psychology, behavioural science is about as apt as "meter reading science" would be for physics.'

But social psychology poses a special problem as an aspiring science, since the situations in which social actions occur are the products of social processes, while the activities of individual actors are the products of cognitive processes. The *psychological* explanation of a certain aspect of behaviour does not have to invoke something special called social psychology, just because the behaviour to be explained is social behaviour, any more than a special meteorological psychology would have to be created to explain why someone put up an umbrella, or an automative psychology to explain how someone drives a car. Human psychology confers many capabilities upon us, and manifests itself in a wide range of activities. We do not have a separate apparatus for every activity we carry out, and so (from the perspective of scientific realism) it would be pointless to have a separate division of psychology corresponding to each activity. It is far more likely that we use much the same psychological apparatus whether we drive a car or play tennis with a friend, and the same conventions of discourse in discussing a friend's moral problems as when we are planning a holiday. The fact that some of these are considered social activities and others not is irrelevant to any kind of psychological explanation. However, we shall see that there are autonomous social processes involved in social action. One could argue that this calls for a sociological component in the explanation of behaviour, or, as we shall propose, that the domain of psychological science be extended to cover processes in which more than one person is involved and which are mediated through conversation and other forms of symbolic interaction. The point about social psychology is only a specific example of a broader argument about research in general and psychology in particular. The real point is that you cannot pick out a *process* for study just by working backwards from a category of observable phenomena or *products*, however clearly that category stands out.

The ambiguity of product–process relationships

In all sciences there are a number of known phenomena – things that require explanation (*explananda*) – and a number of known causes, processes or templates that make up the domain of explanation (*explanantia*). The former are the *products*, the latter the *processes* of their production. Furthermore, it will be known in some cases, but not all, which phenomena originate from which sources. Anatomical structures of plants and animals originate from genes. As the science develops, new phenomena will be discovered and new source proces-ses proposed, while new connections between source processes and the phenomena they produce will be uncovered. The linking of Mendel's Laws of Inheritance with the chemical properties of DNA and RNA is just such a story. On the face of it, a major mode of development in any science would be the picking out of new (that is, as yet unresearched) phenomena, which would then be studied to find their causes or, more generally, their origins. In this way, social behaviour, or particular types of social behaviour, could be selected as topics and traced back to the psychological processes responsible. In many cases, this is just what projects in social psychology set out to do; this is how their purpose is conceived.

But it is just this apparently sensible point of departure that leads to the problems. First, familiar categories of phenomena do not always correspond one-to-one with sensible divisions of the under-lying process. In other words, although every product is produced by a process, the same kind of product is produced sometimes by one kind of process, sometimes by another. This is why there is no 'physics of carpets'. Of course, every feature of every particular carpet is produced by some particular physical and chemical proces-ses, which could serve as an explanation for colour (why *this* carpet is just *this* colour), but there are all sorts of ways of making carpets of a given colour and texture. Furthermore, carpets are human artefacts, and what makes something a carpet is a human convention. So no coherent branch of physics could, in its own right, represent the study of carpets and all the processes that go to make them what they are, taken as a set. To put it another way, carpets are not a *natural kind*. For the same reasons, the psychological explanation for social *explananda* may not form a coherent and profitable topic for a branch of scientific psychology. The same social behaviour may be the product of diverse psychological and social processes; and what is to count as the same type of social behaviour (say, mourning) may be collected up into a category by a human social convention, which differs from one society to another.

Even if we have identified new phenomena (say, the 'risky shift', the tendency for groups to be more reckless than individuals), they do not have to originate from new processes. Very often it will be the case that a new phenomenon, once explained, will be found to originate from well-known source processes. What a shame it would be to expend one's effort trying to account for type D social behaviour, only to find that its explanation involved reference to the very same processes that explained types A, B and C, studied previously.

Finally, because the same product may be produced by different processes, we cannot read off the underlying processes from our knowledge of the products – quite the reverse, in fact. Selecting a product for study does not provide *any* path to the source process. Psychologists have been slow to grasp the point. One *still* sees the statistics of observations offered as causal laws in far too many cases. From a chosen process and knowledge of the conditions in which it occurs, the products can usually be inferred; but, starting from a chosen product, all that may be expected is yet another critical description of the phenomenon – which is not even necessary for, let alone sufficient as, an explanation. We have already seen in the last chapter that it is the source analogue and its associated explanatory model that carries us forward into scientific explanations.

Applying the product–process scheme

For all these reasons the predominant mode of advance in the established sciences has been not the selection of new phenomena for which explanations might be sought, but the conjecture that further processes might be at work whose products could be sought as evidence for the existence or modes of working of such processes.

Consider, then, the effect of asking a rather different question from that which typifies much of social psychology: not 'What is the origin of such and such a type of social behaviour?' but rather 'Given the psychological and social processes we believe to be at work, what additional ones might there be, which have yet to be accounted for, and by what accessible manifestation might we check their existence and properties?' In particular we might seek the *fundamental* processes or principles that provide the basis of all psychological explanations. An understanding of the structural chemistry of DNA *together with* the theory of natural selection has given biology a unified foundation. Explanation requires reference to *both microstructure and macrostructure*, to the biochemistry of organic molecules and the ecology of environmental systems. The theory of tectonic plates *together with* the thermodynamics of the whole earth is the basis of modern geology, while the construction of the atomic nucleus and its constituents *together with* cosmological hypotheses about the history and structure of the whole universe is the basis of physics. Such things are not just arbitrarily chosen items from the explanatory schemes of their respective disciplines, but core concepts around which large areas of knowledge are organized.

Much of psychology will depend, therefore, on a cunning complementation of microstructural and macrostructural explanations. However, the social sciences do not always respond well to the natural-scientific mode of explanation. Whereas the surface phenomena of the natural world seem to rest on stable, tractable explanatory mechanisms and principles, into which enquiries can penetrate for quite a way before hitting the conceptual quicksands below – the paradoxes of time (special relativity) and causation (quantum mechanics), for instance, are at the farthest reaches of our understanding – the social sciences seem more problematic. Surface phenomena may be described individually or collectively, but, as soon as any attempt is made to go further towards an explanatory basis, the conceptual quicksands are found to lie *immediately* below the surface. Problems of the nature of mind, of the reality of free choice, consciousness and cultural relativism: these imponderables are encountered at a much earlier stage in the search for explanatory processes than are the corresponding paradoxes of the natural world.

These are not just philosophers' brain-teasers. Without some resolution of the alternatives they propose, the psychological sciences cannot proceed *at all*. Unfortunately, by adopting the ostrich-like strategy of refusing to address these issues, psychologists have often slipped into building their projects on the sandy foundations of naïve pseudo-resolutions of central problems. If it is the case that social and psychological explanation seems like quicksand, when compared with the 'solid rock' underpinning the natural-scientific landscape, then it will not lend itself to once-and-for-all timeless explanations. Whole cultures may be erected on particular resolutions of the great problems. For Muslims, freedom is conceived of in terms of action rather than decision. In the contemporary United States the problem of agency is resolved in favour of the routinization of many of the activities of everyday life. In these circumstances, the inroads made into the underlying process of social life, the tunnels we dig, will soon deform and collapse, and a different strategy must be used for making progress – a strategy that does not depend on the establishment of structures which are invariant and permanent. Rather, the way of getting about in such a medium as this is to look for points of relative stability, relatively higher 'viscosity', against which leverage can be exerted, if only for the time being. The explanatory task of social and psychological sciences, in other words, may not be to relate ephemeral phenomena to timeless fundamentals and unchanging quasi-physical laws, but to relate what is fast-moving to what is slow-moving, to locate the rapid fluctuations of the social world in the larger and slower progressions within which they occur. This is to introduce a theme that will be argued later on more fundamental grounds: that the central explanatory progression we should consider is from the fast-running fine detail of behaviour and other events, back towards the slower and grosser patterns which, far from merely resulting from the accumulation of micro-events, are the sign of major organizing principles, *by virtue of which* the smaller and faster events occur as they do.

Empirical studies generally may provide one of the forms of evidence by which structural theories may be evaluated, but in themselves they will only test, not generate our understanding of organization. Often it will be the case, as Einstein held, that the theoretical possibilities in a given case are relatively few, and among them the choice can often be made by quite general arguments. Arbitrary hypotheses will not stand in place of coherent theories in this respect.

Hypotheses are worth testing empirically only if they are entailed by, and therefore stand to evaluate, more general theories of sufficient stature to matter whether or not they are true. The experiment is supposed to elicit the underlying process, or its implications, not to reconstruct the original phenomenon. In this respect, the plea for more 'natural' and 'realistic' experiments has been misguided, and has served only to increase the attention given to surface phenomena at the expense of underlying processes. It is naturalistic *observation* under the control of analytical analogues that tells us what the phenomena are. The point of an experiment is *not* to re-create the natural course of events, as has been presumed in much of psychology, but to force a process at work behind the natural events to show its hand in an unusual and criterial way. A 'surface experiment' in which a familiar chain of events A–B is investigated to see whether, under controlled conditions, B occurs if and only if A has occurred is in itself hardly an experiment at all. For this reason there may be no place at all in social psychology for experiments as opposed to model-controlled observation and data collection – though experiments will be (and are) crucial to the study of conscious processes of consultation of rules, of anticipatory rehearsal and of the underlying cognitive mechanisms (information-processing modules) by which people produce social behaviour.

Studies which are not initially part of an overall framework will not usually contribute to theoretical advances after the event. Much of the reason why biomedical and physical research produces a steadily richer and more potent picture of how things work, while social and psychological disciplines only get larger and more fragmented, is that natural-scientific studies are, from the outset, part of an organized conceptual framework, and when completed they contribute to that part of the scheme from which they were derived. Their conceptual significance is guaranteed by their theoretical origins, and is not contingent on the content of the outcome of experiments. With social-psychological research, in particular, though the same point applies to research in personality, the emotions and other fields, studies are often done in isolation from any body of theory, and are therefore from the outset without a framework to which they could be relevant, however they turn out. The pieces of the jigsaw accumulate in journals, despite the fact that a *real* jigsaw can only be made by taking a picture and cutting it up into pieces, not by making pieces and hoping they will form a picture.

The underlying domain of processes by which a science may properly be defined is what we shall call a topic domain. The candidates for such a domain must have certain essential properties if a systematic account of them is to constitute a satisfactory scientific topic. They must in some sense be *concealed*, or else they do not stand to be discovered in any strong sense. Just as there might be cognitive processes unknown to an individual actor, so there might be emergent and systematic properties of the social order, of the kind found in macro-economics, where public and collective patterns of preference and behaviour escape attention by virtue of the scale, pace and complexity with which they operate. This is true even for most micro-social processes, such as family decision-making (see Pearce and Cronen's (1980) pioneering work). It is here that the role of analytical analogues becomes crucial, since they control how the phenomena are abstracted from the complex flow of public events.

The topic domain must also be *coherent* or else knowledge of one part will imply nothing about another. No inferences or chains of reasoning will be possible beyond the unconnected list of primary observations, and no map will be produced on which journeys of imagination and invention can be plotted. Structures and processes in the topic domain must have *causal powers* over surface events, or else nothing in the familiar world would be explained by new discoveries, and no empirical test of conjectures would be possible. The constituents of the topic domain must be *stable*, or at least relatively so when compared with the events to be explained and with the procedures of discovery. If this were not the case, the findings would be out of date before they could be useful, and the very picture itself would be blurred like a moving object photographed with a long exposure, because the pace at which information and evidence for a certain state of affairs had built up would have been overtaken by concurrent changes in the state of affairs itself.

In this connection it is worth pointing out that the concept of a process is being used in two rather distinct senses. An 'occurrent process' is like a causal chain in which later events arise because of earlier ones. An 'existent process' means something more like a mechanism – some device or arrangement (possibly abstract like a set of rules) which, by virtue of its constitution, is responsible for the chains of efficient causation that arise. The latter sense of process is to be preferred, since its referents are generally less ephemeral, and better matched to all the criteria listed here, than are the fleeting wisps of history that make up the set of occurrent processes.

Further, the objects in the topic domain need to be *real* if the science of their description is not to be relegated to the disappointing status of mere instrumentalism – just an empty instrument for predicting the future and retrodicting the past. Finally, the topic domain needs to be a *natural* division of object or process types, and further to be subdivided into other natural units for the purpose of investigation. Failure to comply with this requirement will result in the formulation of pseudo-generalizations, since summary properties will be attributed to sets of causes or mechanisms whose members do not make up all or only the instances that would have important features in common. It is here that source analogues play a crucial role in controlling the way the hidden productive mechanisms that lie behind observable phenomena are conceived.

All of this is by contrast with many of the standard topics in social and personality psychology, the psychology of moral development, of the emotions, and so on, which seem on closer inspection to deal characteristically in surface objects and phenomena, unreal entities, unnatural kinds, observation statements with little if any theoretical foundation or implication, and inductive inference from observation to generalization.

The marriage of ethogenics to cognitive psychology and microsociology

On the face of it, the candidate for a satisfactory topic domain might include the following: the structural and causal properties of the public, interpersonal world, of which a special case would be the social environment or 'society' and the languages and other semantic systems through which it is created; the description of particular networks of relations linking thoughts, feelings, actions and circumstances (a category that subsumes much of present-day social psychology); the abstract forms of these relationships, such as laws of learning and reinforcement, generalized over a wide variety of specific behaviour and situation types; the nature and organization of conscious experience; the 'software' of the brain, which would include cybernetic, artificial intelligence and functionalist topics and modes of enquiry. This is the conceptual strategy by which psychology could become truly scientific. It is very like that of the electronic engineer who studies the parts of a circuit in terms of their function. But it is rather more abstract, since it involves the novel step of transposing the overall functions of the whole system ('I remember . . .') into processes in a memory-organ, a part of the whole system. This analysis would end only in the 'hardware' of physiological description of the brain itself. Of these alternatives, only the last two satisfy the criteria set out above. The immediate contacts of the social world and the stream of consciousness, for example, are surface phenomena; while the abstract descriptions of those contacts *as theories* are but empty instrumentalist versions of the 'one-level world' point of view, in which no recourse is made to real underlying explanatory mechanisms. The truly scientific approach deals in the nature of the real mechanisms rather than just in what they do. Some of these mechanisms are to be found in the information-processing modules of individuals, others in the conversational and other symbolic interactions of social groups. To stop at abstract descriptions of these processes could be to attempt to explain behaviour much as one might explain the presence of daylight by saying that day follows night, and it was recently night. A scientific explanation is based on the hypothesis that the earth orbits the sun while rotating on its axis – that is to say, day and night, winter and summer, are made intelligible by means of a constitutive explanation in which the behaviour of a part of the system is accounted for by the constitution of the system (solar orbit) and the properties of that part (rotating earth).

If we accept this line of argument, and resolve to pursue a form of explanation for human conduct dealing in brain software or hardware (and we should prefer software, for reasons that will be explained shortly), on the one hand, and social, especially conversational, processes, on the other, we are led to the question of what parts and interrelations exist within the joint system of brain software and symbolic interactions we are coming to regard as the mind. Let us suppose that the substructure of the mental system may be inferred, at least to the limits of present knowledge, from the substructure of psychology as a discipline – much as one could infer, from the organization of anatomy books and courses, essentially how the functional organization of the body is divided up. The list of topics that figure in most general psychology textbooks or courses turns out not to be the array of parts from one conceptual scheme, one way of 'carving up the pie', but the interwoven items from four different and largely unrelated schemata.

The first schema suggested by the typical curriculum is what might loosely be called the 'parts of the mind' schema, and this contains such topics as perception, cognition, memory, decision-making, motor skill, and so on. These units might well be boxes in an engineer's blueprint for a natural or artificial mental architecture, and they are in many cases neuro-anatomically localized, in others socially located, as decision-making may be located in a committee. The second schema consists of the epiphenomena, or properties and capabilities, of whole individuals – learning ability, individual differences in cognitive organization, the aberrations of psychopathology, and the like. The third schema differentiates not the various objects of description but the possible types of description. In this schema, the topic domains of physiological and mathematical psychology would be different. Finally, the fourth schema distinguishes populations to which psychology may be applied, such as children, animals or old people. Interestingly, these four systems or conceptual schemata for the infrastructure of psychology suggest that some things we tend to bracket together are really quite different, such as developmental psychology and the psychology of children, or personality as an individual attribute and individual differences considered as distributional phenomena. Only the vigorous pursuit of the strategy we have advocated – namely, ethogenic analysis, at the middle level of experienced phenomena, via abstract description, to a duality of individually *and* socially realized cognitive science – can resolve these difficulties.

In the last chapter we built up the basis of ethogenic psychology by the use of naturalistic models, with analytical analogues and source analogues (theatrical metaphors and rule-following explanations) co-ordinated by the general idea of human life as dominated by cultural conventions and mediated by language. In this chapter we have taken a further step – to define the research programme by which the processes involved can be understood by a repetition of the double-analogue strategy. The analytical analogue is information and its patterns of flow; the source analogue is dual: the software by which that information is processed in intra-individual modules, and extra-individual (or social) structures corresponding to the function that information plays in the story of human mental life created by the ethogenic programme.

In defence of collectivism

Throughout this book we have argued for a three-tier psychology, the middle level of conscious, well-controlled thought and action being dependent on further structures, beyond the range of the actors' explicit knowledge and attention. The basic tier includes 'information-processing modules' which control the sub-routines through which conscious action is implemented. The third tier has both an individual and a social dimension. The one is the deep emotional structure of the psyche, the other the structures of the institutions and other social orders within which we must live and which are the creations of language, culture and history. In this section we turn to the problem of their interrelations and to the question of which has the ultimate priority. Can the one be reduced to the other?

These issues have been very much debated. An important distinction has emerged from the discussion. The question whether the social order itself can be conceived as fully accounted for by the thoughts, feelings, dispositions and actions of its individual members is one issue; while the question whether the social order can be *studied* only by studying the beliefs, propensities and behaviour of its individual members is another. The doctrine that social studies are just studies of lots of individuals is called 'methodological individualism'. The two questions have not always been kept distinct. Some philosophers have argued for methodological individualism by trying to prove the reductionist thesis, which we might call 'ontological individualism' – that social phenomena are nothing but aggregates of individual phenomena. We do not propose to recapitulate the details of this debate, which can be followed in O'Neill (1972) and Lukes (1973). The arguments have turned on whether social processes, such as the maintenance of a class structure, economic changes, such as inflation, and other large-scale social phenomena can be discussed wholly in terms of the psychological attributes of individuals. The question that is of interest to us is complementary to this issue. Are there processes occurring in social groups that should be included in the field of psychology? Perhaps cognition is not a monopoly of individuals but can also be a social process. This matter takes on a developmental dimension, when one considers the possibility that individual minds take on the forms they do under the influence of social factors, like collective ways of making moral judgements or the linguistic forms by which a community expresses self-knowledge. Many writers have urged that the way an individual thinks and behaves is significantly influenced by social processes. George Herbert Mead, for example, forcefully argued that both the self and the kind of knowing we call consciousness are products of social processes, but his suggestions were never followed up with a systematic research programme.

The first issue of substance concerns the possibility of picking out an entity, a social entity, on which to practise psychological investigations. If processes of rational decision-making, of remembering, and so on, could be said to occur in social groups as well as in individual persons, the boundary between individual and society would dissolve. Individualism denies that such investigations would be appropriate to any such entity, though specific forms of association such as families, groups at work or crowds might seem to exhibit autonomous psychological processes. If it were possible to prove that groups, families or crowds were merely surface phenomena and their processes social only in so far as they were surface too, it would follow that the concealed cognitive processes in collectives are actually concealed in individuals, just as they are assumed to be in individual psychology. As such they are not social by nature, although they may be dubbed 'social' by virtue of having exclusively social products. Social products need not have social origins.

To pursue the metaphor of psychology as the study of software, the 'collectivist' would need to show how a programme could be realized and implemented collectively. One possibility would be the case in which each member of the social group takes on the information-processing role of one of the mental modules, the totality of which makes up the cognitive capacities of a brain. One person would do 'remembering', another 'comparing', another 'inferring', and so on. Information flow between the modules is achieved by conversation among the participants. This kind of collectivist psychology is still largely underdeveloped and offers an exciting field for research. Recent work on the way scientific research teams function is suggestive in this regard, but it is still rudimentary. The most advanced work has been on the cognitive processes that occur in institutions (see Argyris 1980).

A weaker form of collectivism would be the claim that there can be social explanations for individual psychological phenomena. These would include the effects of the social world on individual thought, action and feeling. An individualist might argue that this suggestion leads to a paradox. It suggests that individual units (people) take their properties from the whole of which they are part (society). Our natural inclination is to see influence exerted by the parts on the whole, rather than the reverse. Soup is chicken soup if the pieces of meat in it are pieces of chicken; however, it does not follow that whatever one puts in chicken soup will become a piece of chicken. Other examples, however, support the view that the whole can influence the parts. The trees in a wood will depend for their kind and shape upon the kind of wood they are growing in, as well as contributing to the kind of wood it is by the kind of trees they are. In the same way, it has to be admitted that a mutual influence exists between individuals and society, and each is influenced by the properties of the other. But that is not enough to rule out methodological individualism. If the dialogue between the individual and society (in itself a surface phenomenon – that is, something whose properties need to be explained) could be accounted for entirely by organizing processes in the individual, determining both the things in society to which the individual contributes, and the things in society to which the individual is susceptible, a psychologist need look no further than to individual processes. This asymmetry is a basic property of control systems (of which the brain is an example) and of the way they interact with their environment. A thermostatic heating system changes the temperature of a room, and the temperature of the room changes the state and behaviour of the heating system, but all of the interesting control machinery is in the heating system, not in the room and its temperature. The effect of the heating system upon room temperature, and its sensitivity to room temperature, are both grounded in the design and construction of the thermostat, not in anything to be discovered by investigating assorted rooms, and the attribute of temperature which they display so unremarkably. Individualists must argue that society is passive in the way that the room in this analogy is passive – that the pool of institutions, buildings, conventions, social practices, and so on, to which individuals both contribute and react has no autonomous cognitive properties of its own.

A familiar collectivist argument takes the form of pointing out that there are episodes in which individuals become enmeshed which cannot even be described without recourse to irreducibly social concepts. In the study of processes that are part psychological and part social, such as the processes governing the train of events in a case of unemployment or divorce, the social dimensions cannot be eliminated without changing the phenomenon picked out for the study. These cases are intrinsically hybrid. According to individualists they are understood better by the conceptual analysis and reassembly of individually located sub-processes of thought than by the identification and decomposition of mixed domains of individual-cum-collective processes. This claim is based on the idea that each case of unemployment, each divorce, is unique. Divorces do not make up a 'kind', for each of which we would expect a common cause. The levels of generalization that are possible when studying such hybrid but commonplace cases are very restricted. Are *all* divorces psychologically or socially identical, so similar that a general kind of mixed social-cum-psychological process can account for all of them? Evidently not. The individualist concedes the conceptual point but denies the collectivist implication. So long as each individual is in command of the social category of divorce, the class of divorces exists. This is quite different from the case where the class exists because each member is produced in the same way.

The most individualistic of all psychological specialities, and the one most resistant to the incursions of collectivism, must surely be the study of biography. A curiosity that any chosen formulation of the nature of a psychological investigation needs to explain is the oddly self-explanatory quality of life stories and other kinds of case histories. They seem to provide patterns of action and their explanations together in the same package, to raise and solve problems at one and the same time. If social life is conceived as the product of individual psychological processes, this would be seen as a psychological process controlling a psycho-social interchange. The life course of an individual (the public, surface, social object) would represent both the source and the consequences of that individual's nature. It would stand as a record of the input–output history of the person, from which the mediating process, that individual's particular patterns of thought, could be omitted with little loss of intelligibility.

However, that is only to raise a further problem – namely, that of the uniqueness of individual biographies. If the mental system we wish to document is functioning as a kind of generative software, of which the individual's life story is no more than a record of inputs to and outputs from the system, each level in the program structure will be moulded to the requirements of its life situation by a higher-order program responding to changes in the environment. The higher-order program will be subject to revision by still higher-order programs, and so on. Day-to-day plans will be influenced by current projects, and current projects by longer-term ambitions. In this case, it is likely that the organizing principles of any individual personality, at most if not all levels of abstraction and control, will be as unique as the individual life course itself seems to be, and with which they interact. This reduces the prospects for non-trivial general findings about the life courses of typical human beings. Any description of large-scale organization in a biography is likely to arise only under the very specific and rare circumstances in which someone ruthlessly carries through a life plan conceived at an early age. Alternatively, descriptions of overall patterns of life can be generally true only at the expense of being vague and banal. In much the same way, the explanation of a computer's behaviour by reference to its program will usually involve rather empty generalizations about binary systems, etc., or specific details of implementation which are confined to that particular machine. Each machine has a unique interaction history because it has been given a unique set of programs and behavioural tendencies.

Does this leave us without a suitable level of generalization to address with our research? To take a different analogy, the physiological characteristics of individuals vary widely, as do the consequences of those characteristics for health and disease. Although few biological generalizations would be true of all individuals, happily the variations do not occur independently but appear in more or less discrete clusters, an example of which might be pathological syndromes, distinctive clusters of symptoms. Each syndrome has a number of interconnected features, so that, if enough features are detected to establish the presence of the pattern, the others may be inferred, prognoses made and remedies chosen. However, it remains true that no syndrome is possessed by all individuals, and no individual possesses all the component symptoms of a syndrome. The generalizations that can be made are all conditional: 'If someone has hypertension, then it follows that . . .' – but of course not everyone does, and for them it does not follow. The findings that might emerge at best from the line of research an individualistically minded psychologist would advocate would not be universals of human nature but mental 'syndromes' – clusters of organizational features that occur and recur together. When they occur, they can be identified and strong inferences made, but for any one syndrome these inferences will be unjustified for most individuals. The mental syndromes would be hybrids of individual and social, environmental and behavioural features. They might well change quite rapidly with time, in which respect they would differ from personality traits and types. They would be more similar to the diagnostic categories of psychiatry and clinical psychology, but without implications of pathology, diagnosis or cure, and of course much commoner and more varied in type. An example of such schemata might be the system of psychological types suggested by Jung.

Many contemporary psychologists, however, are not convinced that the study of individual cognitive processes, located in this or that human being, could provide the kind of understanding of the range of human actions and interactions that a scientific psychology should provide. We turn now to a statement of the collectivist case – that there are psychological processes that are not reducible to an aggregate of the cognitive workings of individual minds.

The fundamental role of conversation

The most promising place to look for genuinely collective psychological processes is surely in conversation. People talk themselves and each other into declarations of opinion; decisions are often reached by discussion that seems to have a momentum beyond the control of any of the participants; even emotions can be redefined in intimate exchanges. In the dual control of action, social processes form the second pole. In a social analysis of human life, conversation becomes the basic reality.

In studying the physical world we distinguish between space–time and the things and processes that exist in it. Space–time can give us a system of locations for the things described by physics and their interrelating causal processes, which together make up a material world. Is there an analogue for this in the social and psychological world? If we take conversation as the basic reality, what corresponds to locations in space are persons. For many purposes the physical place of a conversational utterance is irrelevant; what matters is *who* said it. The Queen can declare someone a knight almost anywhere, but if one of us were to do so, even in Buckingham Palace, our declaration would be null and void. What corresponds to the causal relations that make up the physical world is conversational interchange, public and interpersonal, in which the intentions of speakers are matched by the understandings of hearers and so create a social 'world'. We should like to think of conversation as located in a grid of 'places' constituted by persons, just as causally interacting things are in a grid of places constituted by locations in physical space. Conversation is a collective activity. Do public conversations have any of the attributes of those private conversations one has with oneself we call 'thought'? If the way we talk to ourselves is a reflection of the way we talk to each other, the public and the private conversation must have common features.

A basic task of the kind of psychology we advocate is to study the relationship between public and private or personal conversations. It is necessary to examine what individual people take from the collective conversation and what they are able to contribute to it. The ultimate project is to discover how far individuals' personal 'worlds' of thought and feeling are reflections of the social world created by the conventions to which they adhere in interacting one with another. So the fundamental idea is of a collective conversation from which individuals take what they need or are encouraged (and sometimes forced) to appropriate.

The difference between traditional and personal psychology can be illustrated by their respective metaphysics of education. According to the traditional metaphysics (see Figure 2), a teacher possesses a large stock of knowledge, while a student has only a small amount of knowledge. Education consists of the teacher passing knowledge from him/herself into his/her student. A traditional examination is an attempt to discover how much each individual student has acquired.

In our theory of education, however, the process is quite differently conceived. There is a general conversation which takes place in institutions like universities, and to which the academic staff contribute. It is from this conversation that students extract what they can. Education, according to personal psychology, is like breathing in the surrounding air; it is not like being pumped up like the tyre of a bicycle.

Figure 2   The wise instruct the ignorant

Individual psychology in relation to collective activities

The array of persons is the 'space' or set of locations for many conversations and other symbolic exchanges. The social psychological world just *is* this conversation. The personal psychological world is created by appropriation of various conversational forms and strategies from that discourse. In so far as individual people construct a personal discourse, they become complex 'mental' beings with individual 'inner' worlds. From infancy they soon cease to be locations of simple utterances which are their unstudied contributions to the public conversation. To develop concepts for making the most of this insight, we propose a psychological 'space' based upon two axes. One axis represents 'display', a dimension marking the difference between those cases in which our psychological states, conditions and processes are revealed in public by declarations of opinion, outbursts of emotion, and so on, and those cases when they are kept to ourselves, 'biting our tongues', 'swallowing our pride', and so on. For example, if one finds oneself in conversation with someone of marked and opposing political opinions, one can hide one's own opinions from the other, in the interests of public amity, and so keep one's convictions entirely private. One neither declares one's views nor lets any flicker of distaste cross one's face. The notion of 'keeping knowledge or opinion private' is more general than the Cartesian idea of mind as a 'subjective' 'inner' realm. There are many ways of keeping things private, of which holding them in an 'inner-subjective' hideaway is only one. The other dimension of our psychological 'space' is 'realization', which marks the difference between individual and collective realizations of some psychological process or attribute – say, reasoning. Is the psychological phenomenon we have picked out for study realized wholly in an individual, or is it fully realized only in a collective, say a family or an army council? We can label this space in the traditional mathematical way, to give us four quadrants. We shall call Quadrant I the realm of the 'social' and Quadrant III the realm of the 'personal' (see Figure 3).

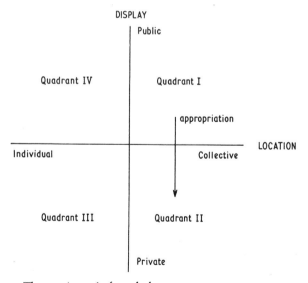

Figure 3   The true 'space' of psychology

The ultimate project of developmental psychology, as we conceive it, is to investigate transitions between these quadrants. We believe that the direction of influence is usually I → II → III → IV → I, etc. In general – and we shall note some reservations and exceptions in the next section – there is a natural priority to Quadrant I: the social or public-collective quadrant. We believe that it is an important advance to see that there are psychological phenomena in all four quadrants.

We have already cited many examples of psychological states and processes that are as much phenomena of public-collective activity, particularly conversation, as they are of individual-private cognitive processing. We would expect to find reasoning in both Quadrant I and Quadrant II. Lev Vygotsky, the great Russian psychologist, was among the first to study the way the forms of public language shaped individual patterns of thought (Vygotsky 1962). As a child develops, the collective conversations which first shape his or her mind are transformed into personally distinctive forms. A child develops an ordered mind first of all by making private some of the public forms of speaking. At this stage the syntax and semantics of thought as private talk are much the same as that of the public conversation. Vygotsky discovered that as children grow up their private speech seems to take on idiosyncratic forms. These are the psychological processes of Quadrant III. Psychiatrists have long been aware that certain patients talk in odd and very personal ways. R. D. Laing (1967) suggested that this kind of talk could be understood if the psychiatrist was prepared to accept novel public conventions for a conversation with the patient. According to the scheme of personal psychology, Vygotsky began the study of the transition of ordered cognitive forms from Quadrant II to Quadrant III, while Laing made some attempt to understand Quadrant III talk when it was publicly produced – that is, transferred to Quadrant IV, the public domain. A great many studies of both Quadrant II → Quadrant III and Quadrant III → Quadrant IV transitions could be done. Some general principles may emerge, principles that would at last come somewhere near representing the minimal conditions for thought and feeling, intention and reflection, to be organized as a mind.

The most important feature that all four realms have in common is language. Only language is both a public and private medium of thought, and only language has the flexibility to expand and develop new forms that are unique to individuals but which can return to the public domain as contributions to an ever-changing stock of conventions.

In a later chapter we shall describe some of the investigations one could make guided by the conceptual structure represented in the diagram in which we have pictured the interplay of the public-private and collective-individual dimensions. The Cartesian scheme sharply polarized the inner-subjective from the outer-objective status of cognitive entities, properties and processes. So it was completely mysterious how we could understand the mind of another person if 'mind' had only inner-subjective status. According to our point of view, however, the 'mind' of another person is spread over the whole of this 'space'. The mind of a poet, inventing and displaying new metaphors, is very much concentrated in Quadrant III and Quadrant IV. The mind of a policeman, representing society in a very stereo-typical way, is represented in Quadrants I and II.

Psychological symbiosis

How are individual patterns of thought and feeling shaped by social conventions? An important aspect of this process is 'psychological symbiosis'. We can illustrate this with the work of Shotter, Newson and other developmental psychologists. The original insight came from the study of tape recordings of long stretches of the talk mothers direct at their infants. These were made by Martin Richards at Cambridge. The analysis of these recordings revealed that most mothers address their infants as if the infants had well-developed psychological repertoires of intentions, wants, feelings and powers of reason from the moment of birth. The mother treated the child as if it was, in reality, what the nature of her speech implied she thought it was. To explain this, Shotter and Newson (1982) appropriated Spitz's concept of 'psychological symbiosis'. It can be illustrated diagrammatically (see Figure 4). The psychological competence of the mother, considered as an individual, is represented by the area of 'M', while the competence of the child is represented by the area of 'I'. The mother does not interact with the child as it actually is but rather with a being of her own invention to whom she has ascribed quite sophisticated thoughts and feelings. The mother reacts to a composite individual, a dyad she herself forms with the infant. This dyad is created by psychological symbiosis or what Jerome Bruner has called 'scaffolding' (Bruner 1983). As time goes by, the dyad changes its internal structure as more psychological functions are taken over by the infant.

This discovery suggests that we might look for psychological symbiosis in other human interactions – for instance, between husband and wife, client and lawyer, and so on. It is our belief that

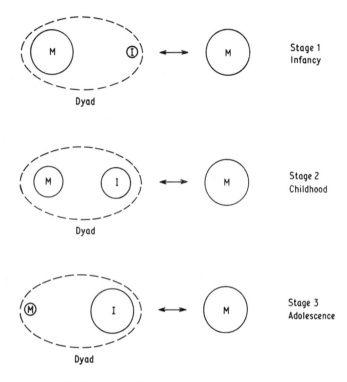

Figure 4   Psychological symbiosis

human beings rarely appear as psychological individuals. They are usually in symbiosis with others, each supplementing the various psychological defects of the other. We believe this to be a ubiquitous phenomenon. It appears, for example, in the work of David Pendleton on what happens when a doctor is consulted by a mother and child (Pendleton and Hasler 1983). His material shows that the doctor does not deal directly with the person who is ill but interacts with a complex dyad in which the other person in the pair contributes to the psychological basis of the performance of the patient, relative to all sorts of social and collective conventions.

A huge research area is opened up by the idea that psychological symbiosis is a widespread phenomenon among human beings. It throws into grave doubt the usual effective isolation imposed on people who take part in psychological experiments, particularly in the fields of social and developmental psychology.

This raises an intriguing question. J. S. Bruner (Bruner and Garton

1978) has drawn attention to the mother's theory of what a child ought to be. That theory, in accordance with which she creates her infant as a person, may be related to general social conditions. David Ingleby (1970) has suggested that there is a connection between the theories that mothers use to 'manufacture' people and the needs of contemporary systems of material production. It would be very interesting indeed to make a comparative study of the 'people' theories of mothers in widely different social and cultural conditions. This opens up the possibility of cross-cultural and inter-class studies, which might look for relationships, if any, between cultural and economic conditions and the specific theories that can be found in analysing the talk by which mothers create symbiotic dyads.

5 WHAT METHODS WILL BE NEEDED TO BRING AN ADEQUATE PSYCHOLOGY INTO BEING?

We have now explained in some detail why a 'new psychology' is called for – why cognitive psychology is not enough for the job – and we have introduced the idea of the priority of social, particularly linguistic, matters over the purely individual. In this chapter we turn to an exposition of some basic methodological techniques built up on the basis of the theoretical ideas so far expounded.

While the experimental method is suited to the investigation of automatic or even of habitual action, other methods are needed to explore the processes involved in deliberate and intended behaviour. The key to this methodology is the act/action distinction. It is as acts that social actions are effective, so any methodology must lead to the discovery of acts. But to perform acts correctly one must know in what circumstances a certain act is called for. By drawing a parallel between the linguists' notion of competence (resources needed for appropriate action) and performance (the use of those resources in action), we can define two tasks for action psychologists. The one is to discover and faithfully represent the body of knowledge actors use in carrying on their activities; the other is to find how this body of knowledge is put to use.

A close study of the kind of talk commonly found as part of human action permits a tentative formulation of hypotheses about social and other forms of knowledge used in psychologically interesting activities, such as self-ascription. Talk is both part of the action and commentary upon the action. In consequence its analysis is a subtle and tricky matter. Further uncovering of actors' resources for action can be accomplished using the methods of repertory grids.

Real-time studies of how actors utilize their knowledge in action calls for a quite different technique. Actors consciously represent only a small segment of the total scheme of means and ends necessary for the guidance of complex activities. An ingenious method, based upon the 'consciousness-raising' effect of interruptions, has been developed to follow out even the most elaborate means–ends schemata in detail.

We emphasize the social and collective status of the bodies of knowledge used as resources by social and practical actors, but much that an individual does is coloured by his or her beliefs about their life course so far. The final step to a complete psychology of human action is the development of sophisticated methods of autobiographical reconstruction – the methods of account analysis writ large.

In the next phase of our discussion we shall build up a methodology and a research programme for a psychology of social action that fulfils the requirements for a genuine science as set out in Chapter 3 and the demands we made in Chapters 2 and 4. In Chapter 3 we distinguished between analytical models and their role in the creation of facts, and the source models and their role in the creation of explanations. We showed the way in which the results of the use of these basic models or analogues come together to form a theory. We also introduced the idea of a structural explanation, based on the principle that the explanation for the structure of a product is to be looked for in the structure of a template. In this chapter we apply these ideas to real problems and illustrate them with some recent social-psychological research. We shall develop a methodology by showing how the ideas of Chapter 3 are to be applied in the scientific study of a social practice, a practice that is based upon a locally valid set of rules.

Automatic versus intended co-ordination of human activity

When a group of people are doing something together, we notice a high degree of co-ordination in their actions. Actions can, however, be co-ordinated in several different ways. There are those cases where the co-ordination is automatic and the actors unaware even that their activity is co-ordinated. There are also cases where people co-ordinate their actions deliberately, knowing not only that their actions are integrated with one another but how the integration is achieved. We can call the first way 'automatic action' and contrast it with cases where people are acting intentionally. Let us illustrate the difference with an example. Peter Collett and Peter Marsh have recently studied how people pass each other in the street (Collett and Marsh 1974). A reader who has not heard of this research may find the results surprising. Although the process of adjusting oneself to other people in the street is seemingly automatic, it is also systematic. Generally, when a man passes a man or woman in the street, the man turns towards the person he is passing. When women pass somebody in the street, man or woman, they turn away. This seems to be a case of automatic adjustment, since the actors are not conscious that they are co-ordinating their movements in distinctive ways. But once people are made aware of such patterns of behaviour they can usually exercise control over them. Their actions may even become rule-governed. For example, most people usually respond automatically to a smile, with a smile. But one may deliberately return smile for smile by conscious reference to a rule of politeness.

We can investigate automatic actions by studying them as if they were part of nature – that is, as if they were the effects of the triggering of causal processes. Some automatic actions are based in a truly natural or biologically based process – for example, returning a smile for a smile. Some have become so engrained that they can be studied as if they were natural patterns of response, such as the utterance of conversational clichés. The proper method of investigating automatisms is the naïve experiment. In simple experiments psychologists try to isolate the causal factors producing some specified response. A good experiment shows that the expected effect occurs in the given conditions but does not occur when those conditions do not obtain.

The actions we perform intentionally, however, must be studied by quite different methods. Consider, for example, the complex co-ordination of actions that make up a marriage ceremony. Everybody who takes part in a marriage ceremony is usually conscious. Indeed, English law now requires that the principal actors in such ceremonies are fully aware of what is happening. This development came about to deal with attempts to escape the immigration laws by forced marriages. In a normal western marriage ceremony, the participants are autonomous agents. Their autonomy is reflected in our belief that, at least in principle, a participant can refuse to go on with the ceremony. There are folk-tales of the bridegroom left standing at the altar, the bride refusing to 'go through with it'. Given this background of assumptions, we look for an explanation of the co-ordination of action in a ceremony by reference to the rules, conventions, and so on, and the deliberate attention of the actors to them. Marriage ceremonies are not part of nature; they are part of a moral order. If any people do not conform to the rules and conventions of a culture, the delinquents can be required to give an account of their actions. They can be reprimanded and exhorted, praised and blamed – not only for their actions but for the kind of account they give of their derelictions and delinquencies. If rules and motives to conform to them or to flout them are the basis of explanations of ceremonial and quasi-ceremonial co-ordinated activities, the method of investigating intentional action must be to try to discover them. Such studies are typically anthropological or ethnographic.

If human social life involved only these two kinds of action production, the automatic/habitual and the consciously rule-governed, there would be no place for social psychology, and the psychology of action would dissolve into physiology and anthropology. We could study automatic processes with naïve experimental methods and we could study autonomous action in the way anthropologists study the culture of a strange tribe. But there is much human action that is enigmatic. We do not know whether it is automatic, whether it is some form of intentional action, or what. For example, when people become friends with one another they seem neither to be merely responding automatically to cues nor to be deliberately following a culturally specific schedule of rule-governed approaches. When people feud with one another, how should we set about uncovering the psychological processes involved? Formerly social psychologists tried to understand enigmatic events by generalizing the method for analysing automatic events. They tried to study helping, friendship, and so on, by experiments. They used scientistic metaphors like 'measure' and 'cause'. While that method and those metaphors are perfectly proper for processes that are automatic or habitual, they are plainly not the correct procedure for studying all human interaction. The method we describe in this chapter is created by generalizing the ways we would use for studying intentional and deliberate action, using known means to pursue consciously formulated goals. But we cannot take the ideas, processes and concepts directly from ethnography into this problem area because as actors we are *not* conscious of the means by which we produce and co-ordinate our actions when we are living 'naturally'. The description and analysis of intentional action provides us with both an analytical model and a source model for *constructing* explanations. So when we talk about agents, rules and rule-following, all these terms are, to some degree, analogical. We are looking for entities and processes that are analogous to them. Methodologically we are following the lead of Darwin, who constructed his concept of natural selection by a careful and extensive study of the similarities and differences between domestic plants and animals and those living, breeding and evolving in the wild. The concept of 'domestic selection' controlled the concept of 'natural selection'.

However, there is one category of human being for which the dichotomy automatic/intentional is exhaustive; and this for a very subtle reason. For very young children, in interaction with their mothers, the two extremes of our distinction – automatic versus overtly rule-controlled actions – are almost all that is needed to understand their activities. The child, taken alone, is almost a pure sociobiological individual. The cultural component of its actions is almost completely provided by the mother. The child, as an isolated individual, does not know any rules or any interpretations for itself. One of the ways of representing social-psychological development is to see the child acquiring, as part of its own store of knowledge, the cultural rules that are, for the first few months of its life, provided by the mother or some other representative of the culture who interprets and controls its actions. We have already introduced the idea of 'vicarious psychology' when we discussed the concept of psychological symbiosis in the previous chapter. In a symbiotic relation, one person creates part of the psychology of another. In the case of the mother–infant symbiosis, the mother is creating nearly all the psychology of the child that pertains to culturally distinctive social action.

The act/action distinction

One of the fundamental principles of ethogenic psychology is a distinction between behaviour, actions and acts. A physical movement or emitted sound can be described without reference to the culture of the person who makes or emits it. In the terminology of anthropology, such a description is 'etic'. We can distinguish mere behaviour into two broad classes: behaviour that just happens, and behaviour that somebody intended (action). However, a newcomer to Italy may be puzzled by a mysterious gesture of the hand, the fingers rapidly opening and closing on the palm. It is clearly not just a movement (mere behaviour) but an action; it is clearly intended. But it is impossible to decide what it means independently of the culture in which it exists. We have to add a third level of description – that of act. As an act, it is a farewell; not, for instance, an invitation to come forward. In the far west of the United States the same gesture means 'speak your mind'. This very elementary analysis illustrates the three levels of an ethogenic description of what people do: as behaviour, as action and as act. In order to make a psychologically relevant analysis of a stream of activity, we must use all three levels. This distinction of levels has a very important consequence for method. It will be impossible to study social psychology – that is, to find the thought patterns behind social behaviour – by studying only action. It will be necessary to identify acts. Part of the methodology developed for ethogenics is a technique by which we can discover the acts that resourceful members of a community take themselves and others to have performed.

One further important feature of the threefold distinction between behaviour, actions and acts is the relations between the three levels. A person can make the same movement (identified by its physical 'shape') and use it for different actions intended for different acts. For example, there is no one-to-one relation between smiling as a kind of bodily movement and the acts we could perform by doing it. It might be a greeting, a threat, an apology, etc. Which act it represents on a particular occasion will depend upon the overall definition of the encounter into which it fits and the kind of episode that is taking place. There are many kinds of acts that can be performed with the same action, and there are many kinds of actions by which we can perform the same act. For example, instead of greeting by shaking hands, in the South Pacific people greet each other by rubbing noses. As behaviours these are very different: each uses a quite different part of the biological signalling system; but the behaviourally diverse actions mean the same thing as acts. It is as acts that actions have social consequences and depend on social antecedents.

In the philosophy of science a useful distinction is made between type and token, and we can draw on it to elucidate the act/action distinction. The idea is very simple and can be exemplified with a physical model. In making coins a single die is used to stamp out a great many pennies. Each penny is an identical token of the penny type. The coins are tokens, and the type is represented by the die. Another way of putting this would be to think of the myriad individual penny coins as concrete realizations of the one penny type. In scientific psychology our interest is focused first of all on *types* of movements, actions and acts. But we have already noticed that the same type of act – say, greeting – can be performed by choosing action tokens of very different types, depending on the cultural conventions of the local society. Only if each type of act had a realization always in tokens of the same type of action (and type of movement) could the one be reduced to the other, in the sense that we could refer to and try to explain the stream of behaviour by considering only actions, and ignoring their force as acts.

Since the act type 'greeting' is not always realized in tokens of just the same type of behaviour, social psychology must study not just behaviour and actions but also acts. Now it is an essential part of the technique of experimental social psychology – at least in the United States – that only actions are studied. The identification of actions as ways of performing the same act is never *explicit*; at most it involves unexamined commonsense assumptions of *local* cultural conventions. We have shown that we need to use the conceptual system based upon socially distinct acts, by means of which we can examine social activity and draw out the relevant actions – those by which socially relevant acts are performed. Unlike the experimentalists, we do not take the act level for granted, but take our own cultural assumptions as a matter for empirical study.

Resources and actions

The second distinction upon which the methodology depends is like the distinction between 'competence' and 'performance' used in linguistics. Linguistic competence comprises the body of knowledge

an ideal speaker-hearer would need in order to produce and compre-
hend the sentences of a language. Linguistic performance is the
actual speaking of sentences on specific, usually conversational,
occasions. We can think of our resources for social action as the body
of knowledge of legitimate projects, rules and conventions appropriate for persons of our sort in specific social situations: 'resources' are
like 'competence', and 'action' is like 'performance'. However, in
many cases the resources necessary for complex social actions belong
to the relevant groups, different members knowing, individually,
different parts of the repertoire.

Linguists, following Chomsky (1967) and ultimately Saussure
(1974), with his distinction between *parole* (speech) and *langue*
(language), have divided the tasks of psycholinguistics along the
same lines. A competence theory is an account of the linguistic
knowledge of a community and how it is organized. A performance
theory is the result of a study of how this knowledge is put to use on
particular occasions for some immediate purpose. Generally, linguistic performances are influenced by, and the speakers take account
of, all sorts of contextual and situational matters additional to the
use of their purely linguistic competence (see Harris 1980). Chomsky
introduced this distinction partly as a way of defining a non-
behaviourist psychological basis for language studies. Any non-
behaviourist psychology must, in a general sense, conform to this
distinction, since it sees speech not as a response conditional on some
regular stimulus, but as the conduct of an actor drawing on a given
body of knowledge to frame a reply which might be quite original.
Using this distinction, we can define two empirical projects. We may
want to discover what an actor needs to know to be able to put on an
ideal performance of some kind – to make friends, to sing madrigals,
to persuade a reluctant shop assistant, and so on. In this context
'knowledge' includes both skills (know how) and matters of fact
(know that). But creating a catalogue of resources does not tell us
how that knowledge is used by an actor or group of actors. There is a
second empirical project – namely, to discover how a body of
knowledge and skills is used on particular occasions for particular
purposes. In linguistics, performance theory is said to be in a very
rudimentary condition, though the now generally discredited trans-
formational grammar of Chomsky was a sophisticated theory of
competence.

We now bring these various distinctions together and describe an
empirical project and the methodology involved to show how an

investigation conceived along the lines we have been advocating might begin.

An example: football 'aggro'

To set the scene, one needs some conception of the events the research project was devoted to trying to understand. It was observed that, during the half-time break at many English football matches, two groups drawn from the supporters of the contending sides assemble behind the grandstand. These groups would confront each other in hostile postures, exchanging insults, particularly by reference to sexual incapacity. It was common for a champion to emerge from each side. The champions would rarely come near enough to exchange blows, but would edge threateningly forward and back, until one had moved the other off the ground. These events, and others like them, were evidently taken with great serious-ness. As a description of those activities, the above is psychologically empty, and yet it sketches a mysterious activity which we would like to understand. To understand it we need first to introduce an analytical model or models. The use of a dramaturgical model opens up a preliminary analysis. But comparing these and other events at football grounds to the staging of a play is not subtle enough; it misses the content or 'plot'. So we add the idea of a ritual as a second, more specific model. In applying these models to the activity loosely described above, we can extract progressively more refined descrip-tions of performance. This analysis will be ethnographic, the result of the use of analytical models by a person who is not a member of the society under study. Social psychologists stand to football hooligans as anthropologists stand to exotic tribes.

The result of this analysis is a description of a sequence of acts/actions. At this stage we have to guess what the acts are. By using our models we hypothesize that those acts have something to do with a ritual, but we do not know what the ritual is *for*. However, people do not *just* act; they talk about and comment critically on their actions. The most important innovation in the rule-based approach to social psychology is the emphasis on the study of that talk. Its analysis becomes an essential part of the investigation. Talk as commentary has two very different functions. In the first place it serves to interpret the actions as acts. The type of interpretation and what happens in the interpretation form a very important part of our understanding, since the status of actions is transformed in the interpretative talk. In the ethnographic description, at the level of action, it emerges very clearly that fans very rarely actually hit each other. In the mid-1970s real violence was rare. But what did the fans themselves *say* about those events? They described them as 'fights'. They spoke of blood, of broken teeth, of the infliction of serious injuries. The newspapers echoed the talk of the fans, creating a 'conspiracy of interpretation'. Why? Because, by being so interpreted, these events are redescribed as socially significant acts. The performance becomes a ritual which marks a step in the course of an honourable career. The outcome is defined as an honour-enhancing 'victory'. In the course of that definition, both winners and losers are created, and as a result the individuals so defined change their status within the social order of football hooligans. The change of status is not the result of the 'fight' but of the *discourse* about the 'fight'.

Interpretative talk is often used after an event to reinterpret the actions to fit with the existing status system. Of equal interest and importance is a second kind of talk that is usually produced only when something has gone wrong with the 'normal' flow of events. This talk is produced to correct or justify imperfections in the first kind of action and talk. Within the second kind of talk one can find explicit rules and conventions for acting correctly. Are they the very rules and conventions which as 'unconscious knowledge' are the true cognitive basis of the production of action? By proceeding *as if* they were, we can finally achieve a coherence test for the *whole* of our psychological understanding. It takes a very long time to collect enough talk at the second level to provide a reasonably full description of the system of rules and conventions. It took Peter Marsh four years to collect enough talk to understand the ritual violence of football fans *as the realization of a system of belief*. Ethnomethodologists have tried deliberately to disrupt social action, to produce artificially the talk involved in 'repair work', but this involves grave moral and technical difficulties. As we shall show, repertory-grid methods make deliberate disruption unnecessary.

Two hypotheses can now be tested. Does our ethnographic analysis truly represent the social reality of the phenomena observed? Is the belief-system we have ascribed to competent participants best described as a system of rules? To test these hypotheses we use our analysis of the second kind of talk, the talk people use among themselves to correct or justify their acts and actions. As we have remarked, this kind of talk is typically produced when something goes wrong, when inappropriate actions are performed or improper acts attempted. On such occasions a senior member of the group displays and/or invokes the rules or norms that should be adhered to in a proper performance of the action. The rules so cited can be checked against the ethnographic hypotheses about the meanings of the actions – hypotheses derived originally from the use of the pair of analytical models.

These accounts of actions are not introspective descriptions of cognitive processes. A human being might be lying about his or her plans or intentions. He or she may not even know what cognitive processes are appropriate for understanding the action. This is quite irrelevant for the analytical use of accounts. In producing their accounts, actors are displaying knowledge of ideal ways of acting and ideal reasons for doing what they have done or omitted to do. On any particular occasion quite other reasons may be in play. Only in the long run and for a whole culture can it be expected that accounts and ethnographic analyses coincide.

So we now have two systems of hypotheses and two sorts of tests. Our first set of hypotheses concerned the partition of the flow of social interaction into actions as the bearers of the acts they accomplish. The first kind of talk tests those hypotheses. Our second hypothesis involves the supposed beliefs of the actors, the implicit rules to which they subscribe, and so on. The second kind of talk tests that set of hypotheses. But that kind of talk was also involved in formulating hypotheses about actors' belief-systems. The final test is whether the whole structure of accounts and hypotheses locks together into a coherent and intelligible combination. There is no 'reality' that could be known independently of those conceptual schemes to which recourse could be made for an 'objective' test. When we collect the accounts from a subculture, like football fans, or a family, or a hospital ward, etc., we search through the accounts for descriptions of what *should* happen. And we *represent* this material as a system of rules *representing a system of knowledge and belief.*

A matrix of socially relevant knowledge

It is convenient to set out such belief-systems in a matrix consisting of four sections: in the first is represented the distinctive social situations which an actor recognizes. For each situation there is a set of rules or rule-like beliefs which the actor must have to be able to act correctly in that situation.

But action occurs on two levels at once. Not only has one to *do* the right thing, but one has to *appear* as the right kind of person. It is no good just doing what a doctor does, for instance; one must appear confident, relaxed and competent. Sustaining the appearance demands a correct expressive performance and the display of the appropriate persona. Research has shown that there are distinctive personae adjusted to each socially distinct kind of situation in which a person acts. Personality is not a simple and constant property of each human being, but rather a presentational style that varies from one situation to another. We shall develop a 'new psychology' of personality further in the last chapter.

It also seems that in each type of situation an actor refers to someone real or imaginary whose reactions serve to express a judgement of the action. In a group of football fans there are one or two older members who act as repositories of propriety and whose reactions are studied by the younger fans. In the work of Marga Kreckel (1981) on the way families converse, a similar phenomenon appeared. The reactions of one particular family member served as the basis for assessing the actions of all the others. In a small nuclear family it is usually the mother, but it can be others.

Studies by E. Rosser show that there are as many as thirteen different systems of action rules and situational definitions known to a single human individual (Rosser and Harré 1976). This conclusion comes from studies of criminals, football hooligans, school delinquents, etc. – not the most sophisticated of social actors. Detailed studies of group systems of knowledge have also been undertaken. Marga Kreckel (1981) has studied the systems of definition and rules for acts and actions through which a family constructs its social life in conversation, and in particular how the status problems created by the appearance of a prospective daughter-in-law in a family were resolved. Kreckel's work closely follows the model described in this chapter. BBC television had made a film of the daily life of a family. Marga Kreckel used the film as the source of representations of the act–action sequences produced by the family. She asked members of the family to interpret, justify and generally account for the actions they severally had performed which were recorded in the film. Two systems of rules for two different kinds of situation emerged. Situations where only the family members were present involved the family's own *particular* set of rules, but where they were interacting with strangers or someone from another family a different set came into use, the knowledge of which was widespread in the community.

In so far as there are different systems of definitions and rules to which different categories of persons (girls or boys; children, adults or the aged; military or civilian) refer their actions, so their social psychologies will differ. From the standpoint of the cognitive psychologist, the same kind of information-processing is occurring in all cases, at least if they occur in a common culture. We have already drawn attention to the social dimension of everything we take as cognitive. Societies and cultures change. Anthropologists like R. Needham (1972), Heelas and Lock (1981) and many others have given us reason to think that there are cultures where even the cognitive underpinnings differ from ours. (For detailed case studies, see Harré (1983).)

Repertory grids

In the method described so far, the analyst depends upon the spontaneous production of accounts. Many important matters are likely not to find mention. Is it possible to go further, using a more systematic, contrived version of accounting? This can be achieved with the method of repertory grids. The analyst uses commonsense intuitions to define a type of situation. The repertory-grid method helps to discover the concepts that people employ in thinking about or acting in that situation. The basic method depends on comparisons of triads. Suppose we wish to study 'being in school' as a type of situation. An important feature of 'being in school' is the teachers. Group the teachers in threes and ask the participants in the study, 'Is Smith more like Brown than he is like Jones?' A participant may say Smith is older than Jones, but not as old as Brown. That participant has used a concept pair (or 'construct'): old/young. The investigator did not invent the concepts whose polar opposition creates the pair; the actors drew on them for a particular cognitive purpose. The process can be repeated by taking more teachers for yet another concept pair, and so on. These pairs form a grid, a repertoire of devices for thinking about and acting in situations of the kind 'being in school'. In the end one has an open but detailed conceptual representation of the cognitive resources available to actors, should they find themselves in that situation. Although it is contrived, it is not a naïve experiment. It exploits a 'natural' way of thinking and acting, because the concept pairs are produced spontaneously by the actors and not imposed by psychologists. There are now completely automated systems, for use with small computers, which not only create the grid but analyse the mathematical structure of the representations.

On the basis of a well-known analysis by T. Mischel (1964), we believe that these repertory grids represent systems of rules or rule-like cognitive entities. As ideal conceptual forms, they control the proper way of thinking about people, situations, or whatever is of interest. They represent a system of rules of proper reasoning about that particular set of objects. It is possible to make multidimensional grids of indefinite complexity. The technique was invented by G. A. Kelly (1955), developed by F. Fransella and D. Bannister (1977), and further elaborated by Mildred Shaw (1980).

Account analysis, coupled with the repertory-grid technique, yields a very detailed representation of the knowledge that an actor must have to perform a certain kind of action and to produce the proper and correct kind of talk. It is a resource or 'competence' study. A very important qualification must be made. The matrix expressing the results of this method represents not the knowledge of an individual person but the knowledge or resources of a collective. When people act correctly and talk appropriately, control is exercised, not by the conditions of individual brains, but by the collective cognitions of the group fractionated and distributed among the members. When Peter Marsh investigated action resources of football fans (see Marsh, Rosser and Harré 1978), he found that no single fan knew everything necessary to produce appropriate action and talk, but he created an informal representation of the rules for creating 'disorder'. His results represent a collective body of knowledge, not an individual share of resources. Two problems remain: how is individual knowledge related to collective knowledge, and how are collective cognitive processes possible? We shall return to these problems below.

Autobiography

We have emphasized that the collective status of cultural resources is shared systems of belief, unevenly partitioned and distributed through a socially differentiated group of people – or perhaps even having only a public and impersonal realization in a book of instructions, a manual. Individuals are born into belief-systems, language communities, and so on, all of which tend to mould people into representatives of a type. But individuals are never exactly alike; each has a unique history. A crucial element in our understanding of each individual is what we know about that person's beliefs about their own past – that is, their autobiography. Autobiographical psychology is a relatively new field, dominated by two main methodological problems.

Perspectivity

Perspectivity is sometimes called 'situation-specific memory'. Different aspects of a person's autobiography are called up according to the 'perspective' from which they are, at the moment, reviewing the past – such as their current emotional state. Depending on the conditions of their recall or citation, radically different evaluations of events are made. (See the work of I. Helling (1976).) In the long run, a person will produce a multiple picture of his or her past life, the richness of which depends on the extent to which the perspectives possible for that person have actually been taken as standpoints from which to recall and order the past. At no stage can an investigator be sure of having identified *all* the perspectives a person might occupy in all conceivable life situations.

Imperfect recall

How is one to distinguish between genuine memories and imaginary events, with all the intermediate grades between verisimilitude and fantasy? This problem has been vigorously tackled by J.-P. de Waele, the leading practitioner of autobiographical psychology. He has developed the method of 'assisted autobiography'. In essence it involves two phases – the first being a reconstructive phase, in which the person under investigation negotiates a compromised personal history with a carefully selected team. The compromise is worked out between his/her initial and circumscribed autobiographical claims and the several proposals for filling out the initial fragments made by members of the team. In the second phase 'problem and conflict situations' are deliberately constructed to prompt recall under well-defined emotional conditions. A typical situation with a specific emotional force is produced. This leads to rapid recall of the details of other situations similar in structure and feeling. The results of the two phases are then combined to produce a final document. (See the work of J.-P. de Waele (de Waele and Harré 1977 and 1979).)

By this means it is possible to find out how much of the collective resources for action are available to this or that individual actor in typical episodes of life.

Methodology for action analysis: the empirical study of performance control

A problem for the psychologist attempting to study the moment-by-moment genesis of action is posed by the fact that an actor's attention is directed almost exclusively to goals or ends, once the actor has any degree of skill. Conceptions of means drop out of consciousness. A solution to this problem might be found by exploiting a phenomenon well known in linguistic studies. When the system for producing action is not working perfectly, some of it is represented consciously. When there is hesitation, we sometimes become aware of how we are trying to proceed, as well as the goal we have been trying to reach. Characteristically, goals or ends are represented together with the steps that are necessary to achieve them. What is the scientific status of such a representation? In the terminology of Chapter 3 it is an explanatory model, an analogical representation of what is going on in somebody's head when they are performing a skilled action. We present ourselves with a *representation*. Whether that representation is pictorial, or takes the form of sentences, or whatever, it is compatible with the possibility that what is represented might be only physiological processes of which we are not currently conscious. Only their structure and interrelationships are represented in this model. When it is in conscious representation, the process appears as an ordered *system* of mental items – like rules, images or goals – which are represented by commonsense concepts. It does not appear as a physiological process.

One does not experience a disturbance in physiology. One experiences a problem about meaning, or about the syntactical representation of what one means, and so on. So, for practical purposes, one can treat the representation itself as a working model. This is the model that M. von Cranach and others have developed for studying the way in which systems of knowledge are put to use in real time by real actors.

The smooth production of action breaks down only accidentally and occasionally. Action psychologists have devised ways of making both practical and social activities break down continuously, to produce a representation in consciousness of most of the system of control, the hierarchy of means and overall and subordinate ends.

Von Cranach has shown that, if one waits for naturally occurring breakdowns, about 40 per cent of the control system is represented; it would be desirable for something like 90 per cent of the hierarchy to be represented. Two methods have been used for creating continuous breakdown. One has been to study people learning a new skill. Kaminsky (1982) has made a very detailed study of adults learning to ski in which, step by step, a control hierarchy of means/end pairs is built up. Von Cranach has developed a method for creating continuous breakdown in the laboratory (von Cranach 1982). With his assistant Steiner he set husband-and-wife teams to work together on a fairly difficult practical project. In many cases a continuous breakdown in the smooth performance of the task occurred because the husband and wife assessed the task in terms of different sub-goals, and of course this led to the choice of different means for achieving the overall goal of completing the task. The clash of goals led to a continuous debate about how to proceed with the project, and so required a representation (in words, in this case) of each step.

The problem that von Cranach and Steiner put to their husband-and-wife teams was how to wrap a baby carriage in paper. A pram is a very complicated thing, and quite difficult to wrap. To make sure that the smooth operation of wrapping broke down, he provided two different kinds of material – one beautiful but fragile, the other strong but ugly. One member of the two-person team would opt for one set of materials, his or her partner for the other. This led, in the 'best' cases, to public discussion and even wrangling about a surprisingly large number of subordinate ends and appropriate means. Von Cranach and Steiner were able to make a representation of the ways that each team member proposed as the best procedure simply by recording the discussion in which nearly every proposed step was debated. To be able to be debated, a step must be consciously represented. In his presentation of the representation von Cranach has reproduced the rival schemes on transparencies, so that one can project one over the other. They coincide at certain points. These points mark moments when agreement was reached and the actual process of wrapping the pram could proceed. Even for such a relatively simple task the schemes are very extensive. They include hundreds of steps, and it is a very tedious process to construct them. It is quite uninteresting to find out how people wrap perambulators. The point of doing this experiment is to test the general hypothesis that a representation of the cognitive processes involved in real-life uses of resources *can* be achieved. This case is on the borderline of ethogenic research and what is now called 'cognitive science'. The items, rules and goals of action are picked out by the use of commonsense psychological concepts, but the hierarchical structures are typical of 'control theory'.

Our late colleague, Michael Brenner, also did some work on these lines (Brenner 1978). He was concerned with a real social problem – the difficulties that arise between old people and the social workers who come to interview them. Many interviews develop into situations of conflict. The social worker wants to find out about the lives of the old people and the old people want to comply with conventions of polite conversation but also to conceal as much of their lives as they feel should be hidden from a prying stranger. The breakdown occurs because of the different social projects of husbands and wives: for instance, an old man wishes to comply with the law, and to answer the questions of the social worker; his wife does not wish to answer those questions, but wants to give the social worker a good impression of the family. Brenner studied the process by which social order is maintained but the social worker is outmanœuvred. Breakdown occurs whenever husband, wife or social worker separately defines incompatible goals for the next phase of the interview. Brenner represented the means–end schemes involved by systems of rules. In a typical episode of this sort, about a hundred or so rules are used, falling into four systems, some of which are general, having to do with people's understanding of the law and of common social conventions, others being peculiar to a particular family. Hierarchies of overall goals and steps to achieve them appear which are similar to those von Cranach unearthed.

These are examples of the use of a source model. The 'production' of social life is conceived to be analogous to the way actors follow a script (which is like a system of rules) to create an illusion of real life. In this way we follow the method of the natural sciences to construct a general theory of social action based on a thesis about a hypothetical mechanism by which action is produced. We come now to the final step in an ethogenic analysis.

Closing the analysis

We have two different representations of the system of rules or, as one could say, the belief-system that forms the resources of the action. We have the account analysis based on the dramaturgical analytical model, which gives us one set of hypotheses about the system of rules. We have another from the action analysis using the actor/script-rule source model, which gives us another set of hypotheses about the system of rules. We can compare and perhaps conjoin them. If they can be conjoined, then a test for the whole system can be developed by trying to synthesize a new piece of social reality. This is the classical method of analysis and synthesis. Techniques such as role-play, experimental theatre, and so on, can be used. In role-play the system of rules discovered in the analytical phase is used to re-create a fragment of social life. Our intuition of the authenticity of the resulting performance is the test for the whole method. The most fundamental analysis of this kind of procedure appears in the work of Mixon (1972), which was very influential in developing the ethogenic approach. Ginsberg (1979) also devoted attention to the conditions of successful role-play. Important, too, is a recent paper by Yardley (1982), which sets out the conditions for the best use of the method. These works should be carefully studied before attempting scenario replications for oneself.

A developmental dimension: acquiring the rules

The method sketched above enables one to find out the rules, conventions and interpretations that are the resources of competent actors. However, it leaves open the question of how the actors acquire their tacit knowledge of the rules. It also leaves open the question of how systems of rules and conventions change. The method provides a foundation for further investigations. Under the influence of Jean Piaget, some work has been done on how children acquire the rules for certain kinds of games. The most famous example is marbles. There is said to be a progression of attitudes to the rules as players become more competent at using them. Much important work remains to be done in developmental psychology, in order to discover how children acquire the rules of social behaviour. The matter is complicated, but recent work suggests that the Piagetian picture of a slow progression through cognitive stages is inadequate. Developmental psychologists have concentrated on studying cognitive developments, it seems to us, because of the general interest in the processes of the education system. Kohlberg's work has been limited by an unwise restriction to a documentary methodology (Kohlberg 1976).

However, recently there has been some more satisfactory study of how the social rules are learned in the period around 8 or 9 years of age. In A. Sluckin's *Growing Up in the Playground* (1981) there is an exploration of the hypothesis that social rules are learned not in the course of disciplined activity in the classroom but in games in the playground. Sluckin shows that there is a close relationship between the rules of the childhood games of a culture and the conventions governing the adult social systems. Children of 6 or 7 do use accounts to justify and comment upon action. Although the children may not be able explicitly to formulate a social rule when asked for it by an adult, it is possible to discover, in their accounts and in their verbal practices of social criticism and control, indications of the existence of rules – rules that are very much concerned with what actions are conventionally permitted. Children on their own behave more like members of a strange tribe than imperfect forms of the adult beings they will become. If an anthropologist went to New Guinea, for example, he or she would not expect the tribe to be able to formulate the rules of life explicitly in answer to direct questions, but would collect anecdotes, proverbs, examples of criticism and praise, and so on. In writing up his or her field notes, it might be that the anthropologist explicitly formulated the rules of that tribe for the first time.

But this will not do for the earliest phases of infancy. Jerome Bruner has used Wittgenstein's idea of a language game, a practical activity with an essential linguistic component, to look for the very first grasp of the idea of a rule. He thinks that in those language games children learn both rules and the idea of rules. (See Bruner and Garton (1978).)

A moral problem

Most people are not able immediately to formulate the rules and conventions they adhere to in social action, in solving problems, in interpreting feelings, and so on. Ethogenics is not based on the stupid question 'What do you know?' Account analysis, ethnographic descriptions, repertory-grid work and action psychology provide hypotheses about social, practical and theoretical knowledge which we have to test, by simulation and synthetic reconstruction. But this introduces a moral element into psychology. If people really were the automata American experimental psychology presumes, this moral problem would not exist. If the conventions of a society are made explicit, there are two effects: some of the power of those conventions is lost, and they become easier to change. One might think it is a good thing to make conventions easy to change, but that is not always true. Marsh's study of violent and aggressive acts among football fans exposed as conventional or ritualized something which, had it been real, would have been physically very dangerous. The wide publicity his work received might have affected the social world by encouraging fans to engage in real rather than symbolic aggression. There are some social activities whose rules of performance it is better remain as implicit conventions. There are other cases where it may be preferable to make conventions explicit, so we can change them. There is no general principle. When we use such a powerful method, we must think very carefully of the social consequences of publishing the results. Events at football matches have become more violent since Marsh's study was published. It is possible that the publication is, in part, responsible. But there are other aspects of social life – for example, the exercise of tyrannical or, more particularly, of bureaucratic power – where it is a good thing to expose the methods by which such power is exercised and the conventions that govern it. Each case must be examined on its own merits.

The examination of co-ordinated human activity reveals two very different kinds of co-ordination. There is the automatic correlation of smiling, turning in the street, etc., and there is the conscious, explicit, literal rule-following of ceremonies, tea parties, and so on. The former may be part of sociobiology, the latter of the study of anthropology. Because there are many kinds of co-ordinated activity that do not fit into either of these groups, however, we need action psychology to try to understand them. The cultural variability of social life suggests that psychology should be non-behaviourist – not a futile attempt to find universal Humean causal correlations. If social life is part of culture, then to understand it we must turn to the study of belief-systems. The methods we have described were successfully used in the analysis of football violence, personality presentation and nicknaming practices, for example, and are among the possible empirical methods for discovering the culturally distinctive rules and conventions of social action. No doubt other methods will in time be developed.

One final qualification: although the ethogenic method is an enormous advance on that of the naïve experiment, we must be cautious in our assumptions about how much 'enigmatic' action we can explain with it. It may well turn out that there will be a need for yet further new techniques.

Up to this point we have treated action more or less atomistically; we have set out methods for finding out how a particular action came to be produced. But actions rarely, if ever, occur as isolated units. Talk, behaviour, thought and feeling *flow*. Conversations are sequences of speech acts, a reverie, a sequence of images and emotions, and so on. Our next question must be 'What are the patterns of action, and how are they produced?' Immediately we raise this question, the world of the thoughts and doings of individual people is left behind. In the typical case a pattern of action and/or talk is created from the contributions of several, perhaps of many people.

The structural point of view

A domain of scientific interest – such as the behaviour of magnets, the life of animals in the wild, human social behaviour or even our uses of language – can be looked at in two very different ways. The individual entities of the domain – pieces of magnetized iron, individual organisms, social actions or single words – can be studied in isolation from one another and from the environment they originally inhabit. This is to treat the domain atomistically. In the anatomical study of animals and plants the bodily forms of creatures are examined in isolation from each other and from their conditions of life. The meanings of at least some individual words can be demonstrated by displaying the things to which they refer. Thus the meaning of 'sheep' can be taught, so it seems, independently of the meaning of 'cow'. But in ecological studies of animals and plants, or in the study of the grammar of a language, the interrelationships between individuals are the centre of interest. For example, the carbon cycle is a complex flow of chemical exchanges between plants and animals. The creatures linked in this way form a kind of system, each having its proper place in the cycle according to its kind. Words find their places in sentences, at least of positional languages, according to their grammatical categories, though it might be more subtle to say that by virtue of their locations they belong to this or that grammatical category; for example, it is place that determines grammatical category in P. Muhlhausler's linguistic games with four-word sentences like 'Grant's Grants grants grants' or 'Ford's Fords fords fords', and so on. In studies like ecology or grammar we treat a domain structurally, since it is the relations between individuals that are the focus of interest. Contemporary natural sciences, like the sciences in the Renaissance, tend to be structural rather than atomistic in style. Should psychology follow this trend? And if it did how would this affect the way psychological studies are pursued?

Psychologists have generally been slow to adopt a structural approach. There are still studies of the emotions based on identifying the physiological reactions of individual human beings. Most surprising of all, much contemporary social psychology is strongly individualistic. This seems to be the result, not of the intrinsic nature of the subject matter, but of two main features of American social life which are reflected in the methodology of social psychology through the recent dominance of the United States in this field. The deep-seated individualism of American culture makes it very difficult indeed for American scientists to conceive of genuine *group* activity. Through the influence partly of individualism and partly of the prevailing 'technologism' of contemporary American culture, an approach called the 'experimental method' has been adopted. Each 'subject' is studied separately and his or her reactions to various treatments recorded and treated as 'data'. However, this cultural dominance is changing. Recent work in developmental psychology (particularly in Britain) has been based on the assumption that human beings grow through their interactions with other people, and this is partly because they function only in interaction with others. We are talking here strictly of 'interaction'; it is not just that one person influences another, but that each person is a working component in a higher-order individual, the pair to which they both belong. In the rest of this chapter we shall concentrate on the case of social psychology, in order to show how a structuralist approach brings out features of social activity which are of central psychological significance, and which the individualistic approaches cannot capture. In Chapter 7 we shall illustrate this point in new ways of studying personality and the emotions.

Preliminary attempts at structural analysis

An obvious first step is to think of a social episode, a sequence of acts–actions, as analogous to a sentence composed of words, phrases, clauses, and so on. In analysing a sentence, one makes use of two analytical schemes: syntax and semantics. One needs both schemes because grammatical categories – based on syntactical types such as noun, verb, adjective, etc. – are determined by general principles of meaning. For instance, the difference between a noun and a verb is not just a formal syntactical difference – that is, a difference in typical positioning in a sentence. It is also a semantic difference, for example between words for things and words for activities. Clearly, semantic and syntactic distinctions are not independent. Research into the structures of social episodes and the encounters therein has been based on an analogy between linguistic syntax and semantics and social syntax and semantics.

The easiest case to tackle is one where the unfolding of a social episode is mediated by verbal exchanges which, taken together, make up a conversation. Research into structure can begin by trying to correlate utterances in conversations in pairs, triads, etc., on the commonsense ground that, just as in the English language adjectives usually precede nouns, so questions might be expected to precede answers, refusals or acceptances to follow requests, and so on. One could use a computer program to identify the units or elements of social events by virtue of their intercorrelations. For example, 'question' is a definite type of act if there is a very high probability that questions are followed by speech acts of the 'answer' type – though sometimes they are followed by another question. But the trouble with a purely correlational method is that it is insensitive to semantic differences, and in particular to speakers' intentions and to hearers' beliefs about those intentions. For example, in English we use statements which have the grammatical form of questions for many different purposes. We can use questions to give orders – a parent might say to a child 'Why don't you eat up your spinach?', not expecting to be offered a reason in reply, but expecting to be obeyed. Adults use questions to issue invitations: 'Why don't we all go to Venice this afternoon?' does not call for a reason for *not* going, but invites a general acceptance. The method of correlations is too crude, particularly if the units we attempt to correlate are identified only by grammatical form. We need a way of identifying distinctive speech acts – that is, examples of types of social meanings – which allows for the complexities of grammatical expressions and their relations to speech acts.

Choosing a theory of meaning

There are two main theories of meaning, one of which has been particularly popular in philosophy. According to one view, meaning is based on denotation: a word has meaning by reference to the thing state, event, etc., which it denotes. Thus the meaning of 'green' is the hue it refers to. Another theory, developed in linguistics, is a structural approach: a word is conceived to have a meaning by virtue of its relationships to other words, the system being anchored only here and there to extra-linguistic reality by denotative relations. For studying language we believe that both theories are needed. But in studying social actions we cannot use a referential or denotative theory. The reason for this emerged in J. L. Austin's work on performative uses of language, or speech-act theory as it has come to be called (Austin 1962). When someone makes a promise by saying 'I will take you to the beach this afternoon', that very act of speaking *is* the promising. It does not refer to some extra-linguistic reality, a promising that might, for example, be in my mind. There is no distinction to be drawn between saying 'I promise' and promising. It is not at all like the relation between the word 'horse' and the four-footed animal it denotes. We must therefore use a non-referential theory to understand the meanings of actions and the uses of words to perform actions. A structural theory has obvious advantages. We have begun to develop the meaning theory of Ferdinand de Saussure (1974) and to apply it to the analysis and understanding of social action.

To give a full account of meaning, it would be necessary to represent in one great map all the relations, both syntactic and semantic, between all the items in a semantic system – an impossible task in practice. But one can simplify the procedure. One can make a map of a typical social episode in which common sense suggests a certain type of social action will occur, such as persuasion. In the Saussurean theory, these maps or representations are called 'syntagmata'. Suppose we are interested in discovering the social meaning of saying 'Thank you'. We can find many orderly social episodes in which this phrase occurs. Sometimes it will be followed by 'Don't mention it', and at others by 'No: thank *you*', and so on. 'Thank you'/'Don't mention it'; 'Thank you'/'No: thank *you*', etc., are 'ordered pairs', Saussurean syntagmata. But there is another dimension in Saussure's theory – the dimension of paradigms. In English-speaking cultures there are many alternatives to 'Don't mention it' which preserve the social force of the episode. For example, in the United States there are 'Ah, ah!', 'You bet', 'You're welcome', and so on. Indeed, in most cultures there is a variety of ways of performing the social act of minimization, including gestures such as a short, sideways cut with the hand. In each of the possible evocations of the act, and thus in each of the possible syntagmata, the possibility that one of these alternatives may be used will be different. Formally speaking, we can say its appearance will have a different probability. If the exchange occurs in England, the probability of the substitution of 'Ah, ah!' for 'Don't mention it' is very low. But the probability of finding 'You're welcome' as an acceptable substitution for 'Don't mention it' is slowly growing.

There are two useful paradigmatic axes for analysing social meaning. On one axis are the substitutions that would leave the meaning of the whole event the same. For example, in England, when a man is greeting a woman whom he knows well, he could shake hands or he could kiss her cheek. The substitution of the one for the other would make little difference to the force of the social event. But there are substitutions which would change that meaning. For example, in England it is not customary for a man to kiss a woman's hand, nor for one man to greet another by kissing, though this last is proper in Italy. For a man to kiss a woman's hand in England would turn the greeting into a joke. This set of paradigmatic relations presents some problems for Poles in English society: Polish men kiss women's hands and the natives want to laugh. For social meanings in English culture the kiss on the hand will lie on the second paradigmatic axis, as a substituand which would change the meaning of the social event in which it is inserted. According to this version of Saussurean theory, the total meaning of a social action is the set of social acts it can be used to perform. The layout of the relations of a social action on the syntagmatic and paradigmatic axes, the Saussu-

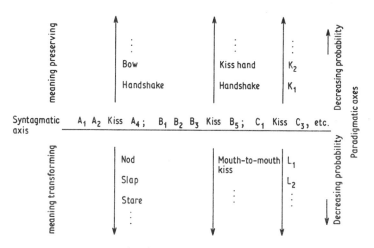

Figure 5   Part of a Saussurean grid for 'Kiss'

rean 'grid', is a representation of meaning. A suitable mathematical representation of the grid is not easy to develop. Unfortunately the only mathematical model that seems anything like adequate is the matrix algebra typical of quantum mechanics in which temporal changes in probability assignments are represented by multiplying a column vector into a matrix. Although the Saussurean grid is clumsy, it does provide a clear but complicated representation of the meanings of elements of intended social interactions. In addition, it allows one to make a non-intuitive selection of real elements from the components of a social episode, provided one can make the first move and pick out provisionally distinctive social *acts* (see Figure 5).

Identifying acts

Speech acts and their force

The Saussurean system gives us a strict analysis only if we can presume we know what the elementary social acts are. We must find a way of determining more exactly what are the acts. How does one know that a remark in the form of a question was an order? What is it to give an order as opposed to asking a question? We can find an answer to these questions by making further use of our linguistic analogy. Austin distinguished between the various forces of speech acts: the locutionary force, the illocutionary force and the perlocutionary force. For example, the expression 'You stupid idiot!' has a certain locutionary force, its literal meaning. An idiot is a person of very low intelligence. In the above context of reprimand a literal reading cannot be intended. In that context the term has an illocutionary and perlocutionary force. In English it is used as a reprimand or as an accusation; these are its possible illocutionary forces. *In* saying 'You stupid idiot!' I am reprimanding you. But a reprimand may have further consequences. It may make you blush. It might improve your standard of work. It might make you leave the room. So *by* calling you a stupid idiot I make you blush, improve your work, make you leave the room. These are perlocutionary effects of the utterance, the consequence of its illocutionary force.

We can take our analysis of social meaning a step further by using this range of distinctions to identify acts by reference to their forces, as revealed by the consequential events in the social episodes in which they occur. We shall identify the illocutionary force by means of the immediate effect of the performance of the action; and we shall identify the perlocutionary force by reference to the expectations and commitments that are created by it. If someone says 'Why don't you marry me?', they do not expect an answer 'Because you are too poor and besides you are too ugly', but 'Yes' or 'No'. If the respondent replies with a reason, this is evidence that they have not taken the question as a proposal of marriage – that is, there has been no illocutionary uptake. In this and similar ways we can use fragments of intuitive understanding to build up a grasp of social meaning. We can study the immediate effect of a speech act or gesture or whatever it is that is done to perform the action by reference to the structure of other social acts which occur in the episode. If the respondent says 'Yes, when? Tomorrow?', then we are entitled to the informal hypothesis that the question was taken as a proposal of marriage. But we can also make use of the expectations created by the perlocution- ary force of the speech act. We know that someone interpreted your utterance 'Why don't you marry me?' as a proposal of marriage if two or three weeks later they begin to complain that they have not seen you since. There would be an expectation that if it were a proposal of marriage she would see him or he her. The system of culturally grounded expectations of consequential events would serve as a further analytical clue to the social meaning of the act.

This example illustrates another point of vital significance. The social act does not exist without two people – a speaker (actor) and a hearer (interpreter). The action *intended* as an act by the actor has to be *interpreted* as an act, perhaps the same act, by the hearer. From the point of view of social psychology, the only thing that matters is the joint act, the product of interpretations and intentions. But in personal psychology what matters is the intentions of the actor and how these are related to his or her belief-system and, independently, the interpretations and beliefs of the interpreter. We must make a firm distinction between social and personal psychology with respect to meanings. In social psychology intentions matter only in so far as they are understood.

Hierarchical organization

Many psychologists have remarked on the hierarchical character of human activity. By this we mean the way smaller units of social action are organized into larger units from which they gain their significance. For example, a war is a gross unit of social interaction. It is bounded by an outbreak (sometimes just an act of aggression, but sometimes by the formalized ritual of a declaration) and by victory and defeat, with a formal act of surrender as a terminus. But it is comprised of smaller units, manœuvres, battles, skirmishes, etc., each of which is composed of yet smaller units, and so on. The significance of the smaller units, however, depends on the structure of the whole. The importance of a battle can be seen only in the context of the whole war. By using the act/action distinction and a generalized version of the illocutionary/perlocutionary distinction, we can specify very precisely the structure of the action hierarchies we find in the episodes of everyday life. Acts provide the organization. A marriage ceremony is picked out of social reality as a unit by reference to the accomplishment of a certain higher-order social act, which itself is a cluster of subordinate acts, each cluster comprising the actions required to perform each subordinate act. At the lowest level are action steps, the intended movements whose components have no independent meanings, and which are distinguished one from another purely by physical criteria.

Act structures and the preservation of selves

We distinguished between the use of a sentence in question form as a proposal which could be accepted or refused ('Why don't you marry me?' – 'Yes' or 'No') from its use as a request for information ('Why don't you marry me?' – 'You are far too poor', a reply which presupposes a prior refusal). There is an important difference between the social effects of accepting or refusing on the status of the parties. We can use this difference to pick out those acts that are 'accountable': that require justifying or excusing by the giving of reasons. For example, an invitation 'Come and have a drink' or 'Would you like a drink?' is accepted with 'Yes, thanks', and no reason for accepting is required. But a refusal, at least among English speakers, must be followed up with an explanation – such as 'No, thanks, I'm driving' or 'No, thanks, very kind of you, but it's a bit early in the day for me'. Refusals are accountable. Casting a request in the form of a question, one presupposes, as it were, that a refusal would be an accountable action. In general an action is accountable if merely performing it would in some way impugn the honour of the person who has been refused. There is then a subtle reason for expressing requests, invitations, etc., as questions. It suggests that the parties' honour is being sustained.

All social interaction, including conversations, is double-levelled.

There is the process of acting and communicating which, in its simplest forms, is common to both human beings and animals, the upshot of which is generally something practical like sharing out the food. But there is something that, although not unique to human beings, assumes predominance in human interactions – a second level of interaction which is concerned with the preservation of or attack upon honour and status, the defence or subversion of selves. This has been called 'expressive activity'. Human beings customarily and routinely produce two concurrent performances, one in the practical and one in the expressive order. It is part of the job of the social psychologist to disentangle them.

Methods of empirical study

According to the new viewpoint, the basis of social psychology is to be found in the formation of hypotheses about the belief-systems that actors need to possess in order to be able to produce the actions they do produce with the meanings these actions actually have, and which the actors intend. Part of the body of social knowledge that must find a place in belief-systems is knowledge of the way episodes are put together – that is, the structure of exemplary forms of typical episodes. Some of the rules which express that knowledge must govern the order in which acts and their actions are produced. We can form hypotheses about those rules only if we know what structures – what orderly sequences of actions, meaningful as acts – are produced by those taking part in typical episodes. We turn now to set out some methods by which the act–action structure of social episodes can be systematically studied.

Computer analysis of sequences

Any sequence of actions or other events can be analysed using a basic three-step procedure. First the stream of activity has to be divided into discrete units, rather as one might parse a sentence. Then the units have to be classified and each event in the recorded data represented by the type or class to which it belongs – that is, actions are classified by reference to the acts they are used to perform. Lastly, the orderly succession of types making up the pattern of events has to be summarized as a sequence of acts. In the simplest kind of structural research, we assume that the kinds of speech acts recognized by investigators are identical with those intended by actors, that the significance attached to them is the same. For 'subjects' drawn from the same social background as ourselves, this is not unreasonable. One can simplify the research method still further by making the somewhat less plausible assumption that patterns of social action will develop in similar ways independently of the social episodes in which they occur. It has been shown by Marga Kreckel (1981) that some such patterns do exist, but that most patterns are specific to the type of episodes and to the particular group of people engaged in the conversation.

However, even with these rather gross simplifying assumptions, interesting results can be achieved by having subjects arrange the speech-act categories provided by the investigators to form hypothetical but plausible sequences; for example, 'plea', 'rejection', 'apology', 'repeated plea', 'acceptance', and the like. The participants can also be asked to indicate where changes of topic might occur and where whole conversations could begin and end. The resulting sequences of event-types can then be fed into the computer for analysis. The results can be quite surprising. For example, in some recent research (Clarke 1983) we had expected that types of social acts would follow a pattern called 'Zipf's Law', whereby event-types would decline in frequency in direct proportion to their rank frequency, whereas the observed relationship turned out to involve the square-root of rank frequency. Our analysis also showed that the likelihood that a conversation will end starts to increase markedly after a certain time has elapsed, but that topics within conversations seem to have no natural 'time span' and their possibility of ending does not suddenly increase, however long they have been going on.

The types of speech acts with which a research project starts can be reclassified into larger family groups on the basis of similarities and differences in their patterns of use. A kind of 'map' can be drawn up showing the most commonly used sequences set out rather like a street plan, on which the joining and parting of ways represents the ways in which different patterns of events can converge upon similar implications for the future, or arise from a common past history.

This takes us some way towards our objective of representing in a single, coherent, systematic 'grammar' all and only the permutations of events which would have meaning within a particular system of behaviour, and thus accounting for the structure we find in the episodes that frame our social encounters. The next step is to try to discover how sequential patterns are produced.

Anticipation and planning

Again taking the very straightforward case where the social encounter is carried on as a conversation, we can ask how much the history of a dialogue influences the choice of each utterance. It also seems important to know whether anticipations and plans for the future of the conversation are taken into account in deciding what to say at each moment. A study of the length and accuracy of the plans of conversers can be carried out in the following way. Pairs of participants can be allowed to converse freely, but one of them has been given a special utterance to be worked into the conversation. To ensure that this is done smoothly, a third party observes the speakers, and the trial is aborted if he or she manages to identify the inserted utterance. As the conversation unfolds, the speaker who is to make the insertion works a device to record moment by moment how long he or she thinks it would be before the insertion could be made. Signals from the device can be used to produce a graph comparing the time expected to elapse against the real time. Once the insertion has been made and marked on the chart, it is possible to construct a perfect prediction curve, showing the subjects' expectations as always being equal to the real time left to elapse. The actual prediction curve could then be compared with this ideal to show how the subjects' accuracy of anticipation changed as the event grew nearer.

Some research using this method has been done in Oxford. There was indeed a dog-leg in the prediction/time curve, indicating an improvement in prediction as the event approached, but it was surprisingly late and small. This may have been due to the highly simplified and schematic nature of the study, in that no episode was specified in which the conversation was supposed to be occurring. We would expect very different results for an interrogation, a lovers' quarrel, a schoolroom lesson, a plenary session in a Politburo, etc. Much interesting research on anticipation remains to be done.

But a pattern of action might emerge in an episode because there is a pre-existing rule-system which determines the overall structure of the events. How could we test for the existence of such hypothetical rule-systems? By drawing on participants' accounts of proper and improper sequences of events – for example, that it is improper to couple a bid for attention with a refusal to accept an invitation – it is possible to devise a system of rules which relate performance of an act–action to the necessary conditions which a prior course of events, including prior sequences of act–actions, must fulfil. These rules can be used to invent sequences of types of social events (act–actions) which have outcomes not actually found among the situations referred to in participants' accounts. For instance, an episode which terminated in an invitation to meet on another occasion could be subtly transformed so that it terminated in a round of farewells. The test for the plausibility of these hypothetical rule-systems was the willingness or unwillingness of participants to accept the new terminations as socially possible outcomes; for example, an exchange of sarcastic personal remarks is very unlikely to terminate in an agreement to meet again in most western cultures.

In a pioneer study along these lines David Clarke found that there seemed to be two classes of rule necessary for the production and reproduction of acceptable sequences of act–actions. The first class governs events that are expected immediately after a given type of event; for example, a reprimand is followed by an apology (or, more rarely, an angry rebuttal). The second class determines events much later in a sequence, events that can occur if a certain prior set of conditions has been fulfilled, including the non-appearance of act –actions of a certain type; a conversation may, for instance, be closed with an invitation to a further conversation, provided that there has been no prior exchange of sarcasms.

Episodes of conflict

Both von Cranach (1982) and Clarke (1983) have found that episodes in which the participants are in conflict can be studied structurally, but a different method of representing structure is desirable. This probably reflects a different kind of rule structure. Each participant has in mind an overall outcome which he or she uses to organize the performance of intermediate actions which accomplish secondary ends. The method involves imagining 'ideal' episode structures from the point of view of the various participants and comparing these with the actual strategies (and tactical moves too) used by people engaged in real conflicts. The results of studies already undertaken along these lines seem to show that two rule-systems are at work, one of which is used to control the overall strategy of the action. This system of rules represents, so to speak, the most logically coherent strategy. However, since the episode is one of conflict, and so one's opponent is also trying to realize a logically coherent strategy, this rule-system can be drawn upon only when the opportunity arises. At other times the actor is concerned to react to, and perhaps counter or neutralize, the efforts of the interactor. The rules of reaction constitute a second-order system of maxims and they interact in complex ways with the strategic rules.

In Chapter 3 we set out the general theory of structural explanation in terms of the different relations that there could be between templates and the products that reproduce their patterns. The examples we have just described illustrate two of the three forms of structural explanation. In the study of the effect of what has already been said on what can be said as the conversation develops, we have a structural explanation of the kind we called an 'assemblage'. There is no overall template on which the structure of the conversation is built up, but as it develops new components, speech acts come to be added in very restricted ways, those restrictions depending on the properties of those which have gone before.

However, explanations in terms of hypothetical rule-systems are examples of the kind we called 'reproductions'. The rules exist independently of the actions they shape, and this is why we have to treat them, in the first instance, as hypothetical. We must test to see whether they really exist. The independence of these rules as templates is vividly illustrated in the example of rule-controlled conflict. The actual pattern of actions produced by the opponents is not a perfect realization of either of their rule-systems, but would not exist in the way it does without the use of both of them.

6 CAN SOME TRADITIONAL TECHNIQUES BE SALVAGED?

The methods of research outlined and illustrated in this book so far look very unlike the traditional entrenched methodologies of academic psychology. The blend of linguistic philosophy, micro-sociology and cybernetics we are advocating needs no five-point scales, no treatment of 'subjects', and statistical analysis is merely preliminary. Is the huge labour of the last thirty or so years to be ditched as worthless, ethnocentric at best, artefactual and illusory at worst? Depressing though the admission must be, we are forced to some such conclusion. However, something can be salvaged, and in this chapter we will explain the ways that traditional methods can supplement and in some places extend the techniques we have so far described.

Intensive and extensive design

In using the method we have outlined, researchers concentrate their attention on what individuals do and say, in order to discover the resources that groups of such people use in carrying on their lives. By carefully examining the accounts people give of their behaviour, the researcher tries to understand the rules of action peculiar to the kind of situation and *kind* of person involved. These rules are susceptible of generalization and can characterize one population in a determinate historical moment. By comparing the rules and conventions of social life from different historical epochs, it is possible to examine their evolution through time.

The basic steps of a scientific research project for many important aspects of human behaviour consist, therefore, in (1) a detailed analysis of the knowledge and skills of each subject and of his/her personal and social circumstances, (2) the extension to wider groups of the empirical results obtained, and of the theoretical considerations tested, in so far as similarities can be established, and finally (3) the utilization by the investigator of his or her knowledge of the rules and conventions of a society, so that each action of a person belonging in the appropriate category can be more properly understood.

In this kind of circular process, data can be picked out only by making assumptions about meaning (for example, what is to count as helping someone), while the patterns in those data can be explained only by theories about the projects and beliefs of the actors. It is impossible to separate data from theories unless one so drastically reduces one's field of interests that there is nothing characteristically human about it. Early attempts to apply the methods of primate ethology to human action suffered from such excessive parsimony. Only theories make it possible to understand actions; and the understanding gained leads, in its turn, to the elaboration of theories and to their confirmation or disproof. The explanation of behaviour is, therefore, an interplay between the formation of theory and the collection of empirical data, best used as in the physical sciences to illustrate the power of theory. The intimate interplay between theory and fact, each dialectically engendering the other, is the most characteristic feature of the natural sciences and responsible, above all, for their development.

It might be objected that observation led by theory can be invalidated by some kind of prejudice, and that better results would be given by 'pure' observation. However, it is a fact that every step in research is supported by hypotheses, concerning both the method and the specific features of the enquiry itself. It is sometimes said that psychology is still a young science, in many ways immature. It presents itself as a loose collection of numerous empirically defined fields not adequately connected with one another – for example, developmental psychology, psychology of the emotions, perception and motor skills. There is an evident lack of those explicatory theories with a wide application which are the pride of 'mature' sciences such as physics and biology (Antiseri and De Carlo 1981). The further away we psychologists feel ourselves from a global understanding of mankind, and the more we realize the limitations of most research in the field of psychology, so much more must we recognize the importance of conceptual analysis, out of which both theory and serious, non-trivial empirical studies emerge.

The elaboration of intensive designs of research has as its final aim the deep understanding, in all its implications, of the actions (including the speech) of the people involved in typical episodes in all their aspects, both individual and social. We shall introduce the idea of the intensive design with two examples. Side by side with techniques known and already tested in psychology – such as observation of behaviour, directly and through films – a special importance is ascribed to less common procedures such as autobiography, and the analysis of actors' accounts.

For one example we turn to a procedure already introduced in Chapter 5, de Waele and Harré's 'Autobiography as a psychological method' (1979). They work out in detail how an individual's autobiography can be elicited by means of a technique that brings together the results of a study (1) of the socio-economic, legal and institutional conditions in which the person lives and (2) of the subject's individual and family characteristics, such as the person's cultural level, his or her place in the family, the conflicts, aspirations, self-conceptions, and so on, that he or she has suffered and entertained from time to time. They also produce examples of the various stages in obtaining the self-justifying accounts which form part of the basic material. Such stages can be defined in the distinction between reflective and direct questions concerning the subject's own life in its various epochs, and in the different methods of the research in use (see the section on 'Autobiography' in Chapter 5). As a psychological research method this is rather complex in its realization, but it clearly differentiates the procedure for obtaining accounts from that of simple interviews.

An example of how an intensive sociological and psychological study – which is at the same time a diachronic and synchronic study of a type of episode rather than a person – can be carried out, is given in Harré and de Waele's 'The ritual for incorporation of a stranger' (1976). They examined the ways in which people introduce one another, in order to find the meaning and structure of the acts involved and to describe the rule-systems by which such ceremonies are controlled in different cultures. First of all, three plays were considered: *Everyman* from the medieval morality plays, Marlowe's *Doctor Faustus* and Shakespeare's *Henry IV*. These provided a background against which historical changes in social practices could be detected. The present 'normal' ways for introducing people in England were described and analysed, and compared with those used in other countries. From these comparative studies it emerged that in the ritual of introductions the social status of the subjects was important. The combined method of ethnographic observation and account analysis showed that the subject's status still has great importance in the rituals of western societies, although it is more marked in some cultures than in others. In all of these methods, research starts with concrete and particular cases, tentatively extended only to a class of cases similar to those with which the research began.

The method we have summed up here is an *intensive design*. The aim is to study concrete belief-systems as they are to be found in individuals or distributed through small groups. The individuals or small groups studied are taken as typical of larger populations. The intensive design is used a great deal in biology. Anatomists study in great detail the structure of individuals typical of their species; ethologists do the same for typical behaviour patterns. Tinbergen did not make a survey of the average behaviour of a myriad sticklebacks; he studied very few very thoroughly.

Much psychology still uses statistical analysis of the results of rather simple manipulations of populations. This is the *extensive design*. The aim is to subject all the members of the group to a treatment (with the exception of a 'control group' which is often left unmanipulated) and average or in some other way blend the reactions of each of the members. The statistical methods used in these procedures eliminate individual differences in favour of stressing central tendencies.

Investigators usually have a choice between the intensive and the extensive method. Each procedure entails consequences and implications of much value. Thus the former, being based on the detailed examination of only a few individuals, allows for a study of each individual in great depth. The use of the intensive method does not create sampling problems. It is very flexible in its techniques and possible conclusions. However, it runs the risk of expending a vast effort on modest and limited results if the individuals studied are rare or idiosyncratic. The extensive method, on the other hand, being based on the examination of many subjects, allows only for limited enquiries about each subject. It must solve sampling problems provisionally, but leads to a quick and standardized discovery of data, and usually allows one to draw conclusions that are felt to have some social importance just because they come from many subjects (Harré and de Waele 1976). The extensive method is most successful if it concerns human attributes that are relatively independent of assignments of meaning – for example, demographic studies, or those relating directly to development of motor skills. But notoriously the extensive design runs the risk of producing results that are trivial or banal. For example, it comes as no surprise to learn that Americans are achievement-oriented or that people prefer to blame their own failures on environmental hazards beyond their control.

The choice between the two designs is connected with very important practical issues, such as the aims of the body that initiated the enquiry and the means at the disposal of the investigator. Rather than using one or the other method, an integration of the two seems in any case to be the better way: if one uses appropriate procedures, it is possible to pick out what seem to be the most typical individuals within a population, and this makes the generalization of the results of intensive studies of such individuals more plausible. A large proportion of the techniques of collecting and analysing data which are commonly used in the social sciences belongs to the application of the extensive method. However, unless one carries out an examination in depth of each subject's individual and social being, the processes 'behind' observable behaviour patterns will never be discovered; instead of achieving a satisfactory *explanation* of human behaviour, one would only reap a list of demographic correlations. The extensive design provides one with samples worth studying by intensive methods.

It could be objected that sampling procedures are on the whole complex and involve a considerable investment of time, numerous assistants and, above all, money. This is only partly true. In fact, there are different ways of selecting elements of the sample, depending on whether resources are limited or whether they are adequate. For example, one could avail oneself of small-scale samplings, or on a larger scale one could apply well-tested methods such as simple random sampling, stratified sampling or cluster sampling (Sudman 1976).

One problem common to all social research is the size of human populations. It is impossible to study *intensively* a very large number of subjects without very considerable resources. Even when manpower resources are available, it is often best to use them cautiously and to limit the number of subjects, otherwise the variability of the human population reduces the amount of detail an investigation can achieve, since the members of a very variable population may have little in common. Therefore, it is often preferable to use alternative procedures to simple random sampling. Since random sampling requires a large population, it can be very expensive to find and contact the chosen subjects. It must, however, be remarked that, the more the research designs depart from that method and employ more complex selection procedures allowing the use of smaller samples, the more is it necessary to know how to control fundamental statistical techniques (cf. Namboodiri 1978) and the characteristics of the population. Since these characteristics are important in relation to the premises and aims of the research, we must not disregard the enormously important role of a powerful theoretical background (De Carlo 1983). In the natural sciences, a theory usually determines the content of the criteria of sample selection. This is especially important for the non-probabilistic sampling criteria in which subjects are picked out by matching them to predetermined criteria, such as 'housewife' or 'elderly'. In these cases the choice of subjects is usually made by considering utility rather than statistical evaluations.

However, we must stress that an intensive design can lead to misleading results if it starts from too rigid a set of theoretical presuppositions. The results must be allowed to modify both the assumption that the members studied are typical, and the attributes assigned to them. The method would lose its necessary flexibility and it would be difficult to achieve authentically innovative results unless the theoretical background was treated as a refutable hypothesis. However, a sampling procedure that does not imply a certain degree of theoretical elaboration is not even conceivable. In fact, the very defining of a population – a starting-point for very many enquiries (not necessarily aimed at the selection of the members of a sample) – requires theoretical assumptions which must be properly thought out. For instance, in order to be able to carry out an enquiry within a certain geographical area, it is necessary precisely to define the area according to ecological, geological, economic and demographic *theories*. Also, we must make clear how we define the human categories involved, such as what we mean by 'fans' or 'group of friends'. Most important of all is the careful unravelling of the theories implicit in the commonsense concepts (for example, of the emotions) by which psychological phenomena are picked out in the first place. Inadequate conceptual analysis has bedevilled psychological research; see Jaspars' and Fraser's (1984) discussion of 'attitude'.

In conclusion, sample selection – a procedure which has its place in the field of extensive designs – can be particularly useful for the chances it offers of extending to the whole population the results achieved through the intensive examination of single subjects, by validating the choice of these subjects or of the particular episodes investigated in depth as typical members of their class or category.

The use of hypotheses in selecting subjects for study makes it necessary to describe in detail the criteria and the techniques by which an investigator has chosen his or her subject population, whether an intensive or extensive design is employed (Sudman 1976). Too often in the course of many researches the explanations that are given are full of gaps and do not allow a serious evaluation of the methodological itinerary that has been followed. Those explanations, therefore, make a generalization of data from sample to class at best uncertain, and at worst impossible.

The place of traditional methods

The range of standard methods

If by 'observation' we mean careful examination of the real world as realized by the senses or by means of the instruments at our disposal, the methods commonly used for the empirical study of human behaviour can be grouped into several categories: auto- and hetero-observation, naturalistic and artificial observation, and experimental manipulation (Segl and Bauer 1975). Let us here concentrate on the procedures and techniques more commonly followed in the psychological field.

By means of hetero-observation one examines human performances such as verbal replies to questions, the act–action sequences defined in earlier chapters, physiological modifications, and in general all phenomena existing external to and/or independently of the researcher, and susceptible to being actually noticed. This kind of observation can occur in 'naturalistic' situations, in which one tries to interfere as little as possible with the subjects under examination and with their surroundings. It is used mainly in ethological and linguistic studies in psychology. Observations of subjects who are unaware of being under observation (e.g. through one-way glass screens) are quite frequent. A part of training in clinical activity includes hetero-observation. The ethogenic method is, in this respect, not at all radical, since it avails itself of the numerous techniques already in use for observing subjects either directly or indirectly via films, tapes, etc., and other methods of recording activity in natural settings. However, it is radical in that it insists that *all* such observation is relative to the assigning of meanings and intentions to the subjects observed, which themselves depend on the often implicit and culturally specific social and psychological assumptions of the investigation.

Auto-observation, on the other hand, consists in the analysis of one's own thought processes, actions, emotive states, and, in general, of one's self in various circumstances. It can be useful to the researcher, both in the preliminary phases of enquiry before elaborating extensive designs, and in the course of qualitative realization of the results achieved through hetero-observation. Care must be taken, however, to ensure that auto-observation should not become a sort of researcher's prejudice, instead of a stimulus for a better understanding of the real world. It must also be remarked that the very placing of this method in a scientific field is often disputed: how, for example, can we state with certainty that some of our mental states can be defined as 'anxious' and not 'aggressive'? Some reductionistically minded psychologists think that in future we shall be able to avail ourselves of appropriate indications of a physiological or neurological order, but this needs an independent, non-physiological criterion based on the subjective correlate. For example, to pick out adrenalin as the physiological correlate of fear requires a prior capacity to pick out our own state of fear from the existing range of subjective states. This requires prior research into folk classifications of the emotions.

Discussion of self-observation and of self-report by some of the more reactionary psychologists has landed them in a welter of confusions which it will be well at this point to disperse.

Can I be wrong (or right) about the mental states I ascribe to myself? Only if I use criteria to decide whether or not I am in a certain state. As Wittgenstein (1980) pointed out, first-person psychological statements are not descriptions that could be true or false, but are avowals that lack criteria. Avowals can be sincere or insincere, but if they lack criteria they can be neither true nor false. To utter or to be ready to utter an avowal is part of what it is to be in this or that psychological state. The same is not true of second- or third-person psychological statements. There are criteria by which I tell whether you are happy, depressed, ruminating or fulminating, and I can be right or wrong about it. This crucial asymmetry in the logical grammar of psychological statements means that most of the 'experiments' of such as Nisbett and Wilson (1977) are just conceptually confused.

Of course I can misapply a psychological concept to myself. I can avow myself as anxious when I should have avowed myself as depressed – when the proper word to have used should have been 'depressed' rather than 'anxious'. This does not mean that I am mistaken about my state, but rather than I have a tenuous grasp of the rules for using part of the standard psychological vocabulary. Furthermore, even if I do have a sound knowledge of those rules, I may on occasion use a word carelessly or inappropriately in these contexts as I may in any other. But that a *community* could be systematically wrong about their uses of psychological words in a public-collective context is logically impossible. It is this logically impossible state of affairs that some psychologists think they have proven experimentally. It is the incoherent assumption needed by Nisbett and Ross to make sense of their way of making sense of their experiments.

Finally, there is a tendency to a confusion of levels. As we have argued repeatedly, there is no sense at all in the idea that all the influences that bear upon human action could be disclosed to consciousness. However, there are powerful reasons for supposing that the all-important 'middle level' of the three tiers of psychological reality must be *wholly* open to human understanding, since it is at that level that our languages are the efficacious organizers and definers of human minds, and from which mental activity acquires its meanings through the social conventions of public use. The lowest tier, which cognitive science explores, and the dual realms of personal and social deep structures to which the attention of psychologists should next turn (see the 'research menus' in Harré 1983) are not consciously represented in the course of the ordinary daily activities of ordinary busy actors. Their representation is the task of scientific psychology. Many of the alleged experimental disproofs of the accuracy of self-description illegitimately generalize the unobservability of processes in the lowest (and sometimes the highest) tier to the whole field of human self-experience. For the time being we must be prepared for as great a variation in our auto-observations as there are human languages. This leads us to consider this method as an important stimulus for the formulation of hypotheses and the explanation of phenomena. As an instrument for a scientific description of the real world it is ineliminable. However, the study of the language of self-description will no doubt become more fully founded, and the possibility of a common vocabulary must remain open, though the evidence so far accumulated tells strongly against it (Heelas and Lock 1981).

In psychology, hetero-observation is often undertaken in artificial situations in which the researcher interacts *somehow* with the subjects being examined, and consequently, willy-nilly, modifies in some measure their behaviour or cognitive state. The mere asking of a question can lead someone to formulate an attitude to some matter which the respondent never had before. The procedures by which hetero-observation is commonly carried out vary enormously. They include the verbal (or documentary) approach, such as the more or less structured interview (whether standardized or not), and questionnaires based on inventories of personality characteristics, for example; the use of scales and tests to record responses and reactions to treatments; and the elaboration of statistical indices of various complexity from the data so acquired by means of techniques such as multidimensional scaling or factor analysis. An important feature of these techniques, particularly when used by those who take seriously the metaphor of measures and statistical elaboration of the same, consists in operational definitions describing a psychological attribute in terms of the test used to identify its presence in a subject; for instance, in order to evaluate a subject's intellectual capacities unequivocally, the score achieved in a certain test may be *defined* as the attribute at issue.

The interview constitutes a very flexible instrument which allows us to notice the interlocutor's behaviours and states of mind, as well as taking in what he or she relates. It is possible to infer both general and specific, both constant and episodic characteristics of the subject who is being examined. It is also possible to organize the interview in a more or less standardized way, and thus obtain information more systematically. (See the analysis of the rule-systems controlling interviews by Brenner (1978).) The more standardized the questions and limited the range of permitted replies, the more is it possible to compare the results of each interview with those obtained from other subjects and in other situations. But this high degree of comparability is achieved at the risk of imposing alien conceptual distinctions on the respondent and turning the results into artefacts. Restricting the range of possible replies presupposes a limit to the kind of responses of which a respondent is capable. What is to be lost in flexibility, however, is gained in terms of comparability between the different pieces of information obtained both in the course of time and in varied circumstances.

Standardized interviews may also be in written form and present themselves as an articulated series of questions in which one tries to limit to a minimum the interaction between the person interviewed and the interviewer. This procedure is called the administration of a questionnaire. It can consist either of open-ended questions or of problems susceptible of objective valuation. In the first case, the researcher will have to develop a way of classifying the results after obtaining the answers, and such a classification will necessarily have a certain degree of approximation and, above all, of interpretation. In the second case, an automatic and precise classification is obtained, since the possible answers are formulated in advance in order to allow the subject only the right of choice between them. The 'closed' method is now in some disrepute, because the items among which the subjects must choose might be ambiguous to the subject or irrelevant to how he or she sees the issues addressed. Preliminary studies are necessary for the sense and clarity of the test material to be evaluated. But even then the results must be accepted with considerable caution. The possibility of comparing answers depends on a diminution of flexibility in the procedure. The most severe limitation of all is that these methods pick up only the subject's skills in dealing with documents – a highly specialized way of conducting interactions, typical of bureaucratic societies. The comparison between an official form and a psychological 'instrument' is no coincidence.

In opinion inventories – and especially in those that aim at studying attitudes – one makes much use of scaling in order to obtain standardized results which are susceptible of a statistical elaboration. There are several techniques of increasing sophistication. One can sometimes avail oneself of 'nominal scales' using easily classifiable characteristics (e.g. classifying the population into whites and blacks or into males and females). In setting up ordinal scales, a rank is assigned to each possible answer, creating a hierarchical continuum – say, from 'least' to 'most', or from 'weakest' to 'strongest'. In interval scales, the researcher assumes that there are equal intervals between the successive steps on the psychological continuum, so that an arithmetical relation can be created between values; for example, one value of a variable may be the double or triple of another. The scalings most frequently used in psychological tests are aimed at analysing specific characteristics of a subject by means of quantitative techniques that yield numerical 'measures'. By means of statistical procedures, the researcher looks for patterns, particularly correlations between and significant distributions of the results. There are statistical tests for validity – that is, whether the correlation reflects a real relation between the attributes studied – and for reliability (for the degree of independence of the results from contingent factors, such as the conditions and the period of time within which the data were gathered). From the point of view of this book, the details of statistical methods are unimportant. The reservations about the scientific values of the methods concern the very way the alleged data are gathered.

The virtues and shortcomings of standard methods

This short survey of current research methods is enough, we hope, to form a basis for discussing their validity as compared with the methods of qualitative research, which in contrast aim at the comprehension of the *generative* processes of human actions, by identifying meanings and intentions and forming hypotheses about systems of belief (the methodology described in detail in Chapter 5).

Looked at from the point of view of their contribution to the problem of explanation of human behaviour, the methods of quantitative measurement, of the statistical elaboration of data and the use of operational definitions of psychological states, etc., are open to serious criticism. Naturalistic observation, auto-observation and the unstructured interview have the advantage of allowing the investigator to penetrate into the thought processes by which behavioural patterns are produced. The direction of probing is under the researcher's control and so leads to the possibility of adjusting the interpretation of behaviour to the persons and conditions involved. Quantitative aims are reproached for rigidity and for self-limitation, particularly because the simplification of the concepts employed makes them unfit for the aim of giving an account of the real world.

An especially glaring example of this failing is to be found in the way that researchers have used the concept of 'helping behaviour' as a universal category. A moment's reflection shows that this includes both 'succour' and 'aid', vastly different in their cognitive background. Much has also been made of the artificial character of the situations that form the conditions of experimental manipulations. These criticisms are very well known and we shall not repeat them here. Suffice it to say that many experiments have created conditions so different from real life as to make them seriously misleading.

At this point we ought to remark that some criticisms of traditional methods are sometimes exaggerated. While recognizing the usefulness of 'flexible' methods, we cannot restrict all the possibilities of enquiry in the psychological field to them. To study the cognitive processes *underlying* any form of behaviour, the *subtle* use of experiments is indispensable. The issue is one of levels. To try to discover experimentally the conditions in which friendships are formed is absurd; but the experimental study of the cognitive processes whereby conventions are implemented, conversational rules fulfilled, and so on, is essential. But should the opposite reaction set in, and methods become too 'flexible' and impressionistic, the opposite danger appears. Once there are serious difficulties in empirical checking, the hypotheses resulting from such methods take us outside the scientific sphere. For example, this happens quite frequently in the field of depth psychology, where Freudian interpretations seem to be indefinitely adjustable to criticism. Of course, we cannot deny the usefulness of what is 'extra-scientific', since today's metaphysics can be a stimulus and impulse for tomorrow's science. What should be emphasized is both the hypothetical and conjectural character of extra-scientific conclusions and the need to subject them to some kind of valid, if indirect, empirical check. Above all, we must beware of thinking that just because we have quantitative methods and numerical results we have achieved the status of a science. Biorhythmics and astrology are also quantitative and numerical!

The ethogenic approach is offered as one example of how the problem of method can be faced effectively. By employing researchers of different cultural and professional backgrounds, we minimize the effect of implicit cultural presuppositions. Great care is taken in how one obtains accounts, in evaluating talk, and in the observation of behaviour. The results are then negotiated between researchers and subjects. Generalization is sceptical and cautious, with an eye to the historical and cultural aspects that differ between one society and another. The hypotheses about rule-sets and inter-pretative conventions can even be tested in performances of ex-perimental theatre. In this way, the method loses its arbitrary features, and at the same time the requirements of methodological flexibility, which are essential in the study of human behaviour, are safeguarded.

The positive side of the 'rigid' methods must also be emphasized. These methods aim above all at creating a form of knowledge that can be wholly public. This is an essential element of modern science. While the complex techniques used to further scientific progress can, in fact, become constrictive and consequently reductive, they do enable the researcher to expand into time and space and make objective for the entire community of researchers what would other-wise remain subjective and contingent. Considered from this angle, the methods of measurement and statistical elaboration, and oper-ational definitions, play an important role. They seem to make psychological theories and empirical results potentially liable to falsification or reinterpretation in the light of new data. Availing oneself of numbers makes information seem more precise and comparison between the results of different studies easier. Through statistical elaboration we seem to be put in a better position to master the relations between phenomena and to draw conclusions about their generality. But all these positive considerations appear to be particularly applicable to research carried out by experiments and in a laboratory. And once again we encounter the problem of the level at which experiments and the laboratory isolation of subjects makes sense. As we pointed out in Chapter 1, there are some bases for suspecting that the whole of this complex of concepts and methods may be of rhetorical value only.

It is far from clear that numerical methods do lead to clarity. Crowle (1976) has emphasized strongly the ambiguity of results: one and the same psychological experiment can be interpreted in many ways. Often researchers bring out only one of them because, by ignoring alternatives, they can show that they have started from a well-defined hypothesis, have tested it and have drawn from it important conclusions. A glaring example of this form of self-deception is the 'Milgram experiment'. Milgram himself interprets his results in terms of 'obedience' (and thus *made* his results fit his hypothesis). Even a superficial study of these results and the con-ditions under which they were obtained shows that 'trust' is a much more powerful explanatory concept in that context. No doubt there are many more 'hypothetical constructs' that would do an equally impressive explanatory job. What, then, was Milgram's 'experiment' testing? If this procedure is accepted, even implicitly, the community of researchers would be responsible for a sort of complicity. A. J. Crowle has also emphasized that research reports frequently fail to describe adequately such essential elements as the characteristics of the population being examined, the sampling procedure used, and *exactly* how data were obtained. In order to overcome the various drawbacks Crowle suggests that experiments should be divided into four phases: designing, running, interpreting and describing. Several researchers should co-operate in the four phases in order to check that no important details are omitted in the description of the experiment, to confirm the quality of the research design and its realization, and to examine the validity and completeness of the available repertoire of interpretations. It must, however, be remarked that these suggestions are likely to prove unpopular, since, in spite of the element of co-operation, they would make current research procedures, which are already quite complex, considerably more complicated, and their results markedly more equivocal. These consequences are unlikely to appeal to those interested in advancing a career!

In what might be regarded as a last-ditch defence, Argyle (1978) has claimed that many of the traditional methods have some substantial validity, even if not free from criticism. In a survey of methods of individual testing, he remarks that the techniques of semantic differential, factor analysis, repertory grid and multidimensional scaling are today much employed also in the field of clinical psychology and, side by side with more flexible techniques, make their contribution to the qualitative study of human behaviour. With regard to laboratory experiments, he also remarks that utilization of interviews, inventories and scalar techniques after the experiments makes it possible to check on the existence of distortions due to laboratory conditions. But to save the 'experiment' by re-establishing the complexity of the real world renders the whole enterprise redundant, since one must already know how psychological phenomena *really* occur in order to assess whether an 'experiment' distorts them.

An eclectic methodology

Having surveyed the advantages and limits of traditional methods in psychology, we can outline some conclusions. In general, the physical sciences use a correspondence between the different magnitudes which characterize real phenomena, and sequences and structures of numbers which represent these magnitudes. On the basis of this correspondence it is possible to operate only in the field of numbers and to describe their properties in terms of algebraic functions. Measurement and statistical elaboration are, in fact, very widely used in the natural sciences. They make it possible to avoid the manipulation, often very problematic, of raw empirical data, and to obtain results by means of correlation techniques, factor analysis, etc., though this 'inductive' approach is very rare in physics or chemistry. But it is not sufficiently emphasized that the measures commonly employed in natural sciences, and to which many of their developments are due, are *indirect* measures of reality. We must take into account the theories at the basis of measurement processes. Even a simple measure like a temperature determination is related in a very complex way to the energy of molecules of which it is a measure. Unfortunately, psychological theories which should link the numerical constructions and the attributes measured are often defective or contradictory. So far as we know, there exists no psychological theory to explain *how* answering the questions of an experimental instrument is related to the cognitive attribute 'attitude', for example. One cannot deny important results in various fields, such as the field of perception, but these are precisely the fields in which theories of measurement actually exist. Thus, those who avail themselves of measurements in psychology must constantly remember that data are *signals* of reality, indices, of which one can avail oneself in order to grasp the processes of human behaviour only if one is in possession of a theory that links those data with the reality of which they are indices (De Carlo 1980). Just as no medical science can exist if it is confined to symptoms, in the same way psychology must not limit itself to the field of statistical results.

The ethogenic method – as we have already remarked above – presents itself as an essentially non-numerical research procedure whereby a precise definition of concepts and the criteria for their application replaces the often illusory sharpness conveyed by numbers. It is concerned above all to exhibit structural properties of mind and action. Mathematical analysis of structures falls into the field of lattice theory, topology, Boolean algebra and other non-numerical mathematical specialities which are currently not part of the curriculum for psychologists. Traditional methods of research can, therefore, offer little to those interested in the mathematical representation of structure. The value of statistical methods remains that of showing how some feature is distributed in a population. Their utility in the search for explanations is marginal.

In this connection it must be emphasized that the ethogenic method was developed partly to improve the scientific status of psychology, but also to revive the connection between areas traditionally linked with psychology, namely philosophy and sociology (Volpato 1982), aiming at a more complete and realistic research of the nature of mankind.

Backman (1979) has suggested that the material which can be analysed in the search for the contents of belief-systems need not be confined to the talk collected by participant observation or provoked by the rule-breaking techniques of von Cranach and others. One could also avail oneself of procedures often used in historical and anthropological fields, such as examining diaries, letters, autobiographies and other publications. Ginsberg (1979), in his survey of emerging strategies of research, suggests that, as well as critically using qualitative and quantitative methods, naturalistic observation and films can provide permanent and reworkable materials for analysis.

In the ethogenic view, human beings are conceived as active agents, capable of modifying and adapting their behaviour to the varied circumstances in a manner that no mechanistic procedure can understand and fully explain. This conception, we think, must be extended to the whole of psychological research more widely than has already been done. Progress beyond the present situation can result only from osmosis between the empirical and experimental experiences and the fields of historical, philosophical, sociological, anthropological and ethnographical analysis. The modest level of the general theories that characterize today's scientific psychology can draw some advantages from an interdisciplinary vision, and from the coming together of different methods into a single vein of research.

7 CAN SOME NEW RESEARCH DOMAINS NOW BE IDENTIFIED?

Though it is not difficult to find aspects of human psychology that have scarcely been studied at all, we think that the opening up of some traditional fields should be of more interest than defining esoteric research projects where there can be no basis of comparison with the results of traditional methods of enquiry. (See, for example, the study of nicknames, by Morgan, O'Neill and Harré (1979).) We round off this book with a fairly detailed discussion of two fields of interest where the 'new psychology' leads to radically different research problems and the use of entirely distinctive techniques. These two fields are the psychology of the emotions and the psychology of personality. The former has been dominated by experimentalists, with an emphasis on physiology, and the latter by statisticians, with an emphasis on traits.

The emotions

The priority of vocabulary

In defining a 'new psychology of the emotions', the first step is to take account not only of what is 'leaking' into consciousness from such physical perturbations of the body as raised heartbeat, excessive swelling of the tear ducts, and so on – the contribution of physiology – but also the contribution of the social world by way of the linguistic practices and moral judgements through which feelings are interpreted as emotions. This step makes the *whole* study of the emotions a great deal more culturally relative than it is currently thought to be. It throws doubt on the ideas of people like Plutchik (1980), who have tried to find some small number of universal or basic emotions. The 'new psychology' of the emotions is a special case of the idea of looking at what is going on in the social and collective world for some kind of guidance about what happens in the realm of personal private activities, such as experiencing an emotion. Our approach to the psychology of the emotions begins with the problem of how we should attempt to define a particular emotion – say, benevolence or anger. Essentially we are proposing that instead of asking 'What is the nature of the emotion of anger?' we should first ask, 'Under what conditions do we use the word "anger"?' What is going to count as anger, righteous indignation, sadness, pity, benevolence, etc., in a culture is defined by what the people pick out by means of a conceptual system that is embedded in their linguistic resources. There may be a great variety of conditions which have to be met for the word 'anger' to be used correctly.

It is very important to make the transition to a prior enquiry into the use of words, for two reasons. One is that it opens up the possibility that we may find other cultures using closely related concepts in rather different ways. Indeed, there may be cultures in which there are, under the same 'umbrella', terms whose logical geography takes quite bizarre turns and which we may have some considerable difficulty in understanding. Secondly, reliance on commonsense, unexamined understanding tends to allow a certain number of rather simple emotions to become embedded in the practice of psychology. If one looks at the literature, it appears that the number of emotions actually studied is really rather small. For example, in Pliner, Blackstein and Spiegel (1975) there are reports of studies only of depression, anxiety, anger and lust. Lust and depression are not emotions. Depression is a mood and lust perhaps a bodily agitation. We are left with anxiety and anger. Anxiety perhaps might be admitted as an emotion, but it is a term for a variety of states, some of which are plainly not emotions. So we quickly reach only anger as the archetype of all emotions. Anger has obvious ethological and physiological aspects. This leads to the intellectual anorexia one finds in the work of such psychologists as J. Gray (1971), a focus on one easily studied stereotype. But as we shall show, even this work is radically defective. Other psychologists have offered longer lists – for example, disgust, grief, fear, guilt, hate, hope, joy, shame, shyness, surprise. But these still fall far short of the complex repertoire of emotions recognized in English.

One reason for this excessive limitation in defining the research target is that psychologists have imported their common sense into their professional studies more or less unexamined. To redress this defect we must turn to a study of what Wittgenstein would have called 'language games', clusters of similar ways of using words, to look at the conditions under which a set of emotion terms is actually used.

Let us take the two important 'green' emotions, envy and jealousy. Under what conditions do we use the *word* 'envy' rather than 'jealousy'? At least the following conditions have to obtain, if B is envious of A. A has possession of some valued object x and generally speaking B concedes that A has a right to it, everything else being equal. B, of course, wants x. The reason why B wants x, according to Sabini and Silver (1982), in many cases but not in all, is because A's having x demeans B. This is the case of malicious envy. Finally, of course, we have to add cognitive conditions that B knows or believes those three conditions hold: A might set about minimizing x, or denigrating B, or both. Let us try to distinguish this from our use of 'jealousy'. According to Sabini and Silver one of the distinguishing marks is that we use the word 'jealous' when B is not at all so clear that A has a pre-emptive right to x. A and B may have at least equal rights. Once again B wants x and the cognitive condition has to be satisfied too. Notice we are now beginning to draw up what Wittgenstein would have called the deep grammatical rules of the use of the words 'envy' or 'jealousy'. What does this analysis show? We are not going to get very far with distinguishing between envy and jealousy unless we notice that there is a distinction in the matter of rights. And so reference to a moral order has appeared on the scene, and that moral order is an essential condition for the existence of those concepts in the community. The existence of the concepts, the possibility of the language games, depends upon there being just this moral order relative to the entity x.

Our approach can be illustrated by some recent work by Nadia Riessland. She found that when one small child disputed with another the mothers were unable to say whether their infants were envious or jealous. Nadia Riessland thought at first that that showed there was some conceptual weakness in the abilities of the mothers to make the distinction. We suggested to her a very simple test which she could use to see whether the mothers had an adequate grasp of the concepts of envy and jealousy. Imagine three characters, A, B and C. A sees B and C very jolly and happy together. In the first condition B is married to C. Under that condition the mothers were unanimous in saying that A would be envious of B. In the second condition A is married to C and without hesitation the mothers said A would be jealous of B. What does that show? In our old-fashioned, everyday world, the story raises a matter of rights. B does not have a right to go trotting around making jollification with C, A's wife, whereas in the first case B has that right, since C is his wife.

Here is a very simple illustration of the role of the moral order in the differentiation of the concepts, and the inescapable necessity of studying word use. How do we explain the mothers' original difficulty? Of course the mothers had no idea what the moral order was, or even if there was one with respect to *those children's perception* of the rights of possession of the various objects of dispute. The original question that the investigator framed was ill posed in the context of the moral order of the nursery, which is, as far as we know, both undifferentiated and opaque.

The work of Averill (1980) must be commended as an anticipation of much of what we advocate, particularly his differentiation between anger and other 'red' emotions. He starts with Aristotle's idea that anger is an agitation brought on by some form of moral transgression and then goes on to develop that notion in contemporary contexts. He builds up a theory of the concept on the basis of the local moral order and implicitly depends upon his knowledge of the language game of 'anger' attribution.

The existence of the conceptual system expressed in the logical grammar of our emotion words depends upon the existence of moral orders. The anthropologist Prince Peter of Greece studied the polyandrous marriage customs in the eastern Himalayas. His description of the emotional state of the people is a central part of the study. He noticed that there was no place for applying the concepts envy and jealousy in sexual relations, though they had a role in property disputes.

Summarizing the work of the philosophers on the rules for using emotion words (Bedford 1957) and of the more sophisticated psychologists on the interpretation (Schachter 1971) and the display (Ekman 1977) of emotions, we can set up a four-component theory (see also Leventhal 1980).

1 With many emotions there is a characteristic bodily agitation, though more than one emotion may be related to it. The James –Lange theory arose by concentrating exclusively upon this component.

2 Many emotions are manifested in typical behavioural displays. The study of such displays goes back to Bell (1826) and Darwin (1859). Such displays are strongly influenced by cultural conventions.

3 In some cases the cognitive activity of seeking and assigning a cause for one's perturbations is crucial in determining the emotion one experiences (Schachter 1971).

4 The involvement of the local moral order, both in the differentiation of the emotions and in the prescription of particular emotions on particular occasions (grief at a funeral), indicates a fourth component in the construction of emotions (Sabini and Silver 1982).

Must all four components be present in order for us to be able to apply our emotional vocabulary correctly? We are not asking an ontological question 'What is anger?' but the Wittgensteinian question 'Under what conditions is the emotional vocabulary, e.g. the word "anger", applied?' In some central cases – for example, anger – we certainly would want to say that all four conditions must be satisfied for the word to be applied. There must be that stirring feeling. There is a repertoire of standard displays for each culture. Anger is an intentional concept: we have to be angry at something or someone. Finally, according to Aristotle and Averill, one must have made some sort of moral assessment that the cause of one's agitation is in some way a transgression or interference with one's rights; in some way or other it oversteps a certain moral mark.

Are there cases where we might be convinced that there are only three or perhaps only two of these four conditions which need to be satisfied for an emotional word to be properly applied? To take a very simple case, the emotion of loneliness: Linda Wood (1983) has shown that there is no specific feeling that can be associated with a distinctive physiological state in loneliness. There is no standard display of loneliness. She found that people who claimed to be lonely said, when they explicated this, not only that they were isolated but that they were more isolated than they ought to be. Those who thought they were isolated, but as they should expect to be, did not claim to be feeling lonely. Those who, in terms of the physical proximity of others, were actually less isolated, but thought they ought not to be so, claimed to experience greater loneliness.

We shall sketch out an analysis of two or three more cases because they offer in different ways interesting research material.

Consider the case of pride. Is there a distinctive bodily feeling of pride? Is there a standard display? Certainly there is some sort of cognitive interpretation and there is some moral assessment of one's worth, etc. It is only in the condition where one believes one has been worthy of victory that one proudly exhibits oneself as victor. Notice the language that goes along with pride. We must regard it as problematic and interesting from a research point of view that we use such words as 'puffed up with', 'swollen with', pride. Is it the case that someone who is proud is actually larger in volume? It seems unlikely. What, then, is the sense of these terms? They could derive from a kind of notional display. We expect someone who is proud to display a cultural image of standing tall, as in a military presence. Perhaps we create a quasi-physiological metaphor on the basis of that image. The matter deserves careful research. Hope is similar. Hope is supposed to surge, or spring. Is there a neuro-physiological state of the surging of hope? Our guess is that, search the literature how you may, you will not find one reported. The surging is, we suppose, a metaphor on the way in which hope 'springs eternal to the human heart', and this is a cognitive matter. But we lack detailed empirical work.

Among the less agreeable emotions are ruefulness and chagrin. Rue, of course, is the feeling of regret. But is it a feeling, in the sense that the sensation of swelling of the tear ducts is part of the feelings of grief and patriotic pride? To rue something is to regret it, but what exactly is ruefulness, under what conditions does it appear, and what relation does it have to a moral order? Regretting is clearly a moral notion, so does it have a standard display? Is there a characteristic bodily feeling that goes along with it? Chagrin is another curiosity. Chagrin, we think, could have a characteristic bodily feeling: a feeling of deflated pride. Chagrin is the sort of feeling we get when we have publicly set ourselves into something and then have been shown that the whole enterprise is hopeless or ill conceived. 'Feeling' seems not to be metaphorical in that context. Is there a standard display of chagrin? It seems doubtful. There is certainly an aspect of cognitive interpretation and of moral assessment. Once again, the whole matter deserves careful and detailed research.

A strong relationship between vocabularies and emotions has been hinted at in a great deal of what we have argued so far. If the suggestion that the philosophical analysis of the emotion concepts which are carried by local vocabularies to reveal the deep grammatical rules of their use is to serve as a basis for psychology, we must conceive the possibility that there are culturally diverse emotion systems or repertoires. This follows, since it has been established convincingly by historians and anthropologists that there are culturally diverse emotion vocabularies. We shall illustrate this with four cases.

Cultural relativity of emotions

In the psychological literature of the late Middle Ages and early Renaissance, the emotion accidie occupies a prime place. Thomas Aquinas devotes the most space in his discussion of the emotions to *acedia*, the Latin version of this word. The history of accidie is closely bound up with the conception of religious duty. The emotion first appears with the nickname 'the noonday demon' in the writings of Evragius in Alexandrian times. Accidie is an emotion which is triggered off by a failure of duty or obligation. It can perhaps best be understood by a comparison with the kinds of emotions that affect modern people in those circumstances. Guilt and shame, depending on the particular occasion, seem to be the emotions characteristic of our derelictions of duty. But, in medieval times, failure, particularly of religious duty, led to neither of these reactions, but to a kind of gloom. *Acedia* was associated with *tristitia*, sadness. The relationship between this emotion and the Catholic moral order, of which it was characteristic, is fairly easy to see. In that moral order, failure of duty meant a loss of intimacy with God, to which the appropriate reaction is gloom. Accidie disappears from the repertoire of western European emotions with the rise of the Protestant faith. Within the new moral order, failure of duty was very largely a matter of the relation in which one man or woman stood to another person so that failure of duty was dealt with in personal terms. It is easy enough to see in an intuitive kind of way how accidie was eventually lost from the repertoire as guilt and shame expanded to cover most cases of dereliction.

If accidie is an obsolete emotion, then *amae* should perhaps be called exotic. *Amae* is an emotion which much occupies the Japanese, and some have said that it is for them the most important emotion. There is no translation into English, or any other European language. When Helmut Morsbach (1976) attempted to give an account of *amae*, he was obliged to attempt it by retailing a dozen or so anecdotes, excerpts from novels, and even by showing pictures. Roughly, the idea is as follows. An adult, particularly a man, can adopt as a kind of play a relation of childish dependence upon another adult. This dependence has a 'sweet' quality. In the discussions of marriage brokers the capacity of a bride as a recipient of *amae* from the bridegroom is regarded as an important attribute for successful marriage. Clearly, *amae* belongs in a radically different moral order from that in which we live. Any tendency to *amae* among growing Europeans would have been firmly suppressed.

Why is it, then, that medieval people experienced accidie and Japanese enjoy *amae*? Our hypothesis is that in a Vygotskyan style the incipient feelings arising by nature, so to speak, are differentially emphasized, suppressed and interpreted by the incorporation of a human being into a local moral order. One of the instruments by which these differentiations are brought about is, of course, the available local vocabulary.

There are few, if any, emotions in the English repertoire which are clearly and unambiguously attached to a particular organ. We do have 'that sinking feeling', 'it turned my stomach', 'his bowels turned to water', etc. But our intuition is that these descriptions are of feelings which accompany emotions rather than constitute them. However, other cultures organize the matter differently. The Maoris operate what can only be described as a hypochondriacal system. The structure of the Maori vocabulary is provided by heart, bowel, liver, and so on. To each of these organs is attached a cluster of emotions. For example, *manawa* (heart) is qualified with *keno* (uneasy), *pa* (grudging), *reka* (gratified), *rera* (excited), and so on. The stomach emotions qualify *puku* (stomach), the bowel emotions qualify *nga* (the intestines), and so on. Paul Heelas reports that there are similar sorts of systems to be found in South-East Asia. These systems raise some very interesting questions for the theorist of the emotions. The heavy load of moral force and assessment that is carried by our western European emotional systems, to the extent that we might describe our emotions as prescriptive, seems to be absent, at least etymologically, from the Polynesian scheme. A very interesting research project suggests itself for the further study of Maori emotions: namely, how far the practice of attaching emotions to bodily organs denies the moral implications of their nearest English equivalents.

A final category which is worth some consideration and so far as we know has never been studied by psychologists, is what we might call the 'quasi-emotions'. These are states of being which are closely related to physical conditions of life. We have begun a modest investigation of 'cosiness'. We say we feel cosy, that a particular sort of occasion is a cosy one, that a room with a glowing fire while the sleet drips down outside is a cosy place to be. We call cosiness a 'quasi-emotion' because of its dual location as a feeling and as a description of place. The interest of this quasi-emotion is heightened by the fact that in other European languages similar states of being and environmental conditions exist but they are not identical. For example, the Dutch *gezellig* is experienced in somewhat similar conditions to those in which we would use the word cosy, but our Dutch informants assure us that someone cannot be *gezellig* alone. (Etymologically *gezellig* derives from the Dutch word for 'friend'.) It stands somewhere between the English word 'cosy' and the German *gemütlich*, which we presume is an emotion which arises only in company. The Finnish 'cosy', *kodikas*, derives from the word *koti*, meaning home. It can be applied to rooms, twilight, the social atmosphere, to the behaviour of material things, such as coffee pots, and even to people. For example, a *kodikas* girl is quiet and agreeable in manner. It is clear from the use of the word that it lacks the duality of cosy and *gezellig*, since it does not appear as an emotion. It is a qualification of the environment and not of the feelings of people. Incidentally, the English word perhaps comes from the Gaelic *cosh*, meaning a small hole into which one might crawl and hence be snug.

The upshot of these comments and analyses is the realization that the psychology of emotions is seriously underdeveloped. It has been dominated by the study of those emotions for which there are clear-cut and dramatic physiological accompaniments, easily measurable in the average physiology laboratory of a university. This could explain the enormous emphasis that has been placed on those emotions in whose physiological component adrenalin plays a large part. The measurement of blood pressure and heart rate is a relatively easy technology. But such emotions are a tiny fragment of the enormously complex repertoire with which our civilization operates. So we are in the encouraging position in which Isaac Newton described himself, as having found a pretty shell or two on the beach while the ocean of truth lay all undiscovered before him.

In search of personality

Sociological analysis, dramas, parts and styles

What analytical models would it be helpful to use to make the complex reality of human social relations reveal some kind of structure? There are two which are particularly helpful for grasping the idea of personality. In a general discussion of method (Chapter 3) we explained how an analytical analogue (or 'model') is used to create the data we need for the scientific treatment of some matter of interest. We gave a very brief description of the dramaturgical model. This example will show in rather more detail how that model can be used. To adopt a dramaturgical model is to look at the social world as if it were the performance of a play. We imagine that what we are seeing is not, say, a family quarrel, a lecture, or a violent incident at a football ground, but a dramatic portrayal of a family quarrel, etc., played on a stage before an audience. This first step immediately yields some concepts for picking out the various aspects of the social world. For example, from the concepts appropriate for analysing a performance of a drama, we have the idea of a 'scene', a meaningful place which has been created for the dramatic action. The scene includes a number of different features; the setting, the props and the scenery very specifically define a meaningful arena for social action.

However, a scene in a play also involves a particular set of human relations. When a play opens the actors are not just scattered about the stage; it is made clear that some kind of crisis is imminent, that some situation has to be resolved. For example, a young Danish prince finds that his uncle has poured poison into his father's ear. What should he do about it? We can look at the social world in these terms, but it is important to remember that it is not the only way to analyse social action, since many other analogues can be applied to social reality, each revealing a particular aspect. In this analytical mode, we ask, what is the situation between people present in that setting if the resolution is going to lead to some social action? This helps us to pick out a relevant sequence of actions from the general activity of daily life.

In a play actors follow scripts. Even in improvised drama there is a scenario which tells the participants roughly how to proceed. This suggests the search for implicit scripts and tacit rules as the basis for understanding the stylized and repetitive events that make up much of everyday life.

The actors are playing parts. This means that relative to the script, the setting and the situation an actor has little freedom of action. This extends into the style in which a part is played. If a play opens with the revelation that poison has been poured into the main character's father's ear but then goes on to reveal that he acts firmly and decisively to uncover the culprit supported by his mature and strong-minded girlfriend, then that play is not *Hamlet*. The Prince of Denmark must be gloomy and vacillating, and Ophelia innocent and fragile. In other words, the style must be co-ordinate with the action. We take that for granted in the ordinary formal theatre. *We also take it for granted in ordinary everyday life.* But to a psychologist there should be something here to be carefully investigated. We have to ask ourselves, 'How is it that people in everyday life generally manage to play parts in styles co-ordinate with the spirit which the situation and scene in their culture demand of them?' We are now coming closer to the formulation of a scientific concept of personality. When people are incompetent and adopt inappropriate styles, then all kinds of social and mental troubles appear. In one of J.-P. de Waele's auto-biographical studies (de Waele and Harré 1979), that of a young man who murdered a postmistress, it was clear that the young man lacked just that kind of competence. He understood the script, but he had very uncertain ideas of how he was supposed to play the part. The solution to his dilemma was simply to bash his way out of the situation by reaching for the nearest heavy object.

If we turn to look at our own lives dramaturgically, it is surprising how many different 'parts' one is called upon to play in the course of a week. For each of these parts there is an appropriate style – curt and perhaps overbearing; amiable, soft-voiced and loquacious; and so on.

With the use of another analytical analogue, another feature of social life becomes more clearly visible. We can look at some social episodes as if they were rituals or ceremonials. In the events which are literally rituals and ceremonies, there are fixed parts or roles. In a church wedding ceremony, for example, somebody plays the role of priest, somebody plays the bride, and someone the bridegroom, and so on. These parts are fixed by the nature of the ceremony. But different individuals can come to play them at different times. At a certain parish church there was a wedding every Saturday but it would be astonishing if one heard that the same bride appeared each time. The role of bride is filled by a succession of different persons and the same is true, though the cycle of changes is rather longer, for the role of parish priest. To return to the dramaturgical model. Someone must play the Prince of Denmark for the play to be *Hamlet*, but different actors can take it on. In a sense, parts are roles.

In coming to mark a role as 'mine', we make use of style. A further point about role should be emphasized, since role will be germane to our understanding of personality. Having a well-defined social world can present a problem for individuals. Consider the role of bank manager. The actions of bank managers are highly formalized, even ceremonial. They dress in a serious way. This puts each bank manager in a certain fix. Unless he is very careful he is going to be indistinguishable from every other bank manager. He has to do something to give the role performance a little twist to show that it is *his* particular mode of managing banks. But there are limits to this. He cannot, for example, joyfully throw handfuls of money around. A bank manager may, then, wish to modify the role. What he adds to it is something that one might call style. He does the things he has to do: he wears the clothes he has to wear, but his performance and its ritual accoutrements are modified and modulated by being presented in a special way.

We usually describe the actual performance of parts and roles in verbs and occasionally nouns. We describe the style of performance in adverbs and, more rarely, adjectives. In analysing a description of a piece of social action, identifying the verbs by and large enables us to find out what the speaker takes to be the role and part performances; the adverbs will generally identify the style – for instance, 'she counted the money grudgingly, cheerfully', etc. Identifying the stylistic qualifications is of central importance, because in and through them a role is marked as yours, your particular version of a way of living in a social world. We are now one more step closer to a scientific concept of a personality.

From sociology to psychology

The analysis so far is within the realm of sociology, depending on a micro-sociological view of the social world. How can we transform this into psychology? The basic idea that links this kind of analysis with psychology is that action as performance is controlled by reference, often without conscious attention, to a body of knowledge, that which the linguists call 'competence'. The kind of investigation we have just sketched on the psychology of bank managers, using analytical models, enables us to formulate a competence theory, a description of a common system of knowledge and belief. If we had an adequate performance theory the two would be a psychology. When we have said what people must know we have said something about someone's mental equipment. Only by contrast with this can we detach *personality*, the individual style with which both public and private aspects of prescribed action are performed.

One further qualification is needed. As we have been expressing the matter thus far, one might be forgiven for supposing that the knowledge to which we have referred should be conceived as located in individual 'heads'. For some fragments of social life – say, buying a second-hand car – it may be that it is possible to deduce from a description of the activity what a competent purchaser needs to know as an individual, how the bargaining is to take place, what the cars are worth, who is the salesman, and so on. Sometimes we have to think instead of the totality of the knowledge required as being only partially represented in each individual. In that case a description of the activity using some cluster of analytical analogues represents an ideal competence: a system of knowledge spread over a social collective or group of people.

Sometimes knowledge is not encapsulated in people's heads at all, whether individually or collectively, but is embodied in practices. Of great interest to the student of personality is the practice of giving nicknames, in the way children, bandsmen, army recruits, etc., use nicknames (Morgan, O'Neill and Harré 1979). A mass of social conventions is involved, governing the way people should and should not be, or perhaps more accurately, appear to be. The majority of nicknames like 'Fatty', 'Skinny', 'Brainbox', 'Stinker', etc., are used to tell the group how a proper person is not supposed to be. The outline of the British Standard Child, for example, is like a photographic negative, maintained by ridiculing and even punishing those members who display unfavoured attributes. The practice of nicknaming encapsulates a vast repertoire of social knowledge.

Myth and method in personality research

How do we get from these observations to the scientific study of personality? The scene has already been set for a general theory of personality by the idea that the playing of parts, performing of roles, putting on of styles, reflects the knowledge and conventions embodied in social practices. From these basic ideas we can construct an account of personality.

Most people would be inclined to think that somebody's personality is something they always have, a permanent set of traits. But we have emphasized the amazing extent to which psychologists are enthralled by *unexamined* commonsense concepts. Personality studies (for example, Eysenck 1967) are a particularly vexing case. The bulk of personality investigations have depended on the idea that people have fixed personalities and the job of the psychologist was just to find out what they were. This was the psychology of personality traits, of fixed dispositions, such as extroversion, introversion, neuroticism, and so on. Personalities were defined in terms of lists of such traits. However, as Argyle and Little showed many years ago (1972) the personality one displays depends on what situation one finds oneself in and the people one is with. The commonsense idea does not stand up to careful testing. To get all this straight we need to introduce another idea, drawn from the dramaturgical perspective. This is the idea of 'persona', the public way people present themselves to one another, masks adopted in everyday life. Common sense suggests we should contrast persona with personality, but when one actually studies persons passing through the social world, through a great many situations and scenes, through many settings, playing many distinctive parts, 'personae' and 'personalities' cannot be distinguished. As people pass through distinctive situations, not only do they do different things but they display distinctive personalities by displaying distinctive personae. In some situations they are grave, agreeable and serious, and in others they are flighty, mischievous and inconsequential. In others they are harsh, abrasive and nasty. But it is just the same person who does all these things.

The commonsense illusion of personality as a set of fixed dispositions is easily accounted for. In the same situation we are usually with the same people. We see each other as we appear in that situation. Every time one goes into the bank one is usually dealing with the same tellers. Most people when they go home find the same wives or husbands and the same children, and so on. In the light of the evidence offered, people form theories about each other. The theory is that a person *is* what they *seem* to be in that situation, and that of course is what is ascribed to someone as their 'personality'. Though it is a simple form of theorizing it is very powerful. Because people have such theories they treat each other in the same way, so that each displays an apparently fixed personality to the same other. On a global scale these would seem to be mere personae. One does have a fairly stable mode of personal display in a group of like situations, but what has stabilized it is not some permanent thing about the actor, his or her personality traits, but what is called for by the script, scene, settings, etc., by the drama that is being played.

Empirical research: explicit knowledge of style and skilled manipulation of persona

To illustrate the possibility of empirical work on the 'presentational' theory of personality, we report the studies of Rosser and Harré (1977). The range of personalities people ascribe to other people by virtue of the peculiar phenomenon of the presentation of self as a persona can be presented in a matrix.

Situations	Rules	Personae	Arbiters
S_1	R_1	P_1	A_1
S_2	R_2	P_2	A_2
S_3	R_3	P_3	A_3
S_{13}, etc.	R_{13}, etc.	P_{13}, etc.	A_{13}, etc.

Such a matrix represents perfect social knowledge, probably distributed through a social collective. Research into the structure of this knowledge shows that the key to its organization is given by the recognition of 'scenes'. For an adolescent these might be 'school', 'football', 'coffee club', 'police station', 'on the bus', 'with my friends', etc. We do not know in advance which of these involve truly independent systems of social knowledge, but ideas of scenes with their settings and situations are the fundamental concepts that define everything else. From a performance point of view it seems that people generally recognize the scene and then fit their behaviour to it (Argyle, Furnham and Graham 1981). But sometimes Machiavellian or powerful people can make the scene conform itself to them. Scenes with their distinctive settings and situations are represented by S_1, S_2, etc., in the matrix. We recognize scenes as places in which we are *supposed* to perform in a certain fashion. One way that actions that are required or proper can be presented is in the form of 'rules for acting'. The choice of the 'rule' metaphor is quite natural, since when required to account for their actions verbally people do often refer to rules as justification for what they have done.

Not only must the action be appropriate; so must our presented personae be appropriate to the scene. These we represent as P_1, P_2, etc., in the matrix. Finally, a fourth element comes out quite clearly in this research. There is some individual person or group of people who are referred to by the actors as a check on the propriety of their performances. In school, children tend to refer to a small group of powerful individuals who control the social presentations of the class, sometimes in opposition to the teacher. Marsh noticed the same thing on the football terraces (Marsh, Rosser and Harré 1978). Propriety seems to be expressed in the reaction of particular individuals rather than in a stated set of rules.

How many of these systems of scenes, rules, personae and arbiters are available to an averagely competent person? There seem to be at least thirteen distinctive systems in use among adolescents, and there may be more. The matrix represents a competence theory for an ideally competent person in a particular culture.

To illustrate this approach in detail, we give an excerpt from the personal matrices of Tom and Jock, both very knowledgeable young men. Each knew his own cognitive matrix pretty well and was able to describe it quite explicitly (Rosser and Harré 1977). Here are one or two of the things that Tom knew about the presentation of self.

On the bus one should not do things loudly or suddenly, otherwise people could take you for a show-off

One should change the opinions one presents publicly gradually even if privately convinced they are wrong, to avoid being seen as a fool

– and so on. Tom knew how to appear in public, how to put on the best show, to demonstrate the best persona, to be ascribed the right kind of personality.

Jock disposed of an even more remarkable stock of knowledge. Jock had come to Oxford from Scotland and reorganized the street gangs. He was extraordinarily knowledgeable about persona presentation. He was interested in various notions of 'being hard'. He grasped a very important point about the relativity of personae to scenes and situations. To be taken as 'hard' by one's peers requires a quite different presentational style from that required to appear 'hard' in the eyes of warders in a borstal institution. To appear 'hard' among one's peers, one must indulge in erratic behaviour that they are not able to understand. They believe their leader must be rational, so if he performs irrationally and violently they think of him as 'knowingly hard' in some subtle and very superior way. But to appear 'hard' to warders in gaol, in case any of our gentle readers may need to do so in later life, here are a few tips. It is important to be sour, unforthcoming, to reject all overtures, to be as silent as possible, and to perform consistently. To be hard with one's peers one performs inconsistently; to be hard with one's warders one must be rigidly consistent. However, Jock was tired of prison and he had the idea that to be admitted to a psychiatric ward was going to give him a much more agreeable life. To further this project he was working up the part of paranoid psychotic (that was his own phrase). He had studied the part and believed it involved aggressive fits coupled with obsessive behaviour. His father had been diagnosed as a paranoid psychotic, so Jock recalled his father's behaviour very carefully, including such actions as carefully counting the objects on the table every five or six minutes and becoming very upset if anything was missing.

Highly Machiavellian characters like Tom and Jock have their knowledge very close to the surface in a highly explicit form. Of course, many of us have not thought about our public front very much. We just go wandering through the social world, changing personae as we change our clothes – easy-going, as you might say. But every now and again one is brought up with a round turn by having presented the wrong appearance. At that point our knowledge, or lack of it, by contrast with the ideal knowledge in the collective, does make itself felt. Tom and Jock are unique, but their skilled performances in the pursuit of personal projects are drawn from a common stock. Jock uses a persona from a definition which is part of the repertoire of psychiatry.

The place of the moral order

To complete this analysis we need to introduce another notion which is really rather like personality but importantly different in many ways – the idea of character. A personality is something which in a sense is morally neutral. People display different personalities. We just notice them passing through our social world as if those presentations were marks firmly fixed to the individual. In fact, of course, personalities are put on by us and for us. That people have different personalities is not regarded as a moral failing. Character, however, is morally accountable. It is similar to personality in structure, but there are good characters and bad characters. Moral issues must be related to the existing moral order. To deal with moral orders we need to introduce some very broad distinctions into our understandings of the social world, most importantly that between the practical order and the expressive order.

The distinction works in the following way: Karl Marx and Friedrich Engels (1973) pointed out that even in the most primitive societies work is socially organized. For instance, there is usually some division of labour. Practical life involves a social organization and a social structure, social relations of power between people, and so on. There is a social psychology of the world of work. Veblen (1899) pointed out a little later that there was another, related, but in some ways independent order, which was also socially organized. This was the part of life concerned with the pursuit of honour and the public proof of worth. It too is a life which has a social psychology because it too is a social order. We could call it the 'expressive' order (Harré 1979). At different periods of human history these orders stand in different relationships to each other. In the time of Marx, the early to middle part of the nineteenth century, the practical order realized in the economic system and its attendant social relationships was probably the dominant force in society, but it has long since dissolved. Nowadays it seems that the expressive order dominates the practical. In our society there are all kinds of ways of gaining honour which are independent of the structure of the economic system, but highly influential upon it. We can look at these orders as independent of one another but subtly interacting in various ways. It is in relation to the expressive order that we believe the notion of character appears.

How does the expressive order work? To understand this we need a concept introduced many years ago by Erving Goffman

(1968). In many institutions there are both moral careers and practical careers. As one goes through school or the army, or a time in hospital, one has a career which can be described in terms of growing skills, improving health, and so on. At the same time pupils are sitting exams, passing or failing, patients are moving from one ward to another, and so on. These changes have an effect on one's status in the world of honour as well as ritually marking practical developments. A moral career consists of the stages of acquisition or loss of honour and the respect due from other people as one passes through various systems of hazard characteristic of different social worlds.

In a moral career one aims for respect by risking contempt. Moral careers are lived in particular worlds, defined along particular roads. A moral career does not just happen: it is to a degree managed. In general we manage our moral careers by concealing our failures and displaying our successes. But all this is taking place in the eyes of others. What we build up in this progress through the moral order is character. A moral career creates character: it creates in others the idea that a particular person has attributes and aptitudes of a certain worth. Just as we ascribe personalities to people and believe that these personalities are constant through their lives, so also we ascribe character, and we believe these characters are constant throughout life. If, however, one investigates the passage of a single individual through the social world (de Waele and Harré 1977), it becomes clear that that individual at any given time is passing through several moral careers in different places at different times, with respect to different people. He or she is passing through a different set of hazards, and in consequence different views of that person's character are formed by the others involved. By virtue of different patterns of success or failure, a person is building up a different picture in the eyes of others.

If it were possible to assemble all the ways in which people are thought of by others, the result would be a very complex mosaic, and who knows whether any overall pattern would be found. In practice it would be impossible to undertake such a piece of research. But one can turn the problem around and ask about the competence of any *one* of us to remember who we are, to know how to behave. By looking at what a person has partially represented in his or her own head, or has access to in the collective representation of social knowledge, one can find out about the totality of characters and personalities that a person could display, by finding out what repertoires of performance he or she is capable of putting on. This is the 'presentational' alternative to the naïve theory of personality as a fixed collection of traits or dispositions.

BIBLIOGRAPHY

Antiseri, D., and De Carlo, N. A. (1981) *Epistemologia e metodica della ricerca in psicologia*. Padua: Liviana.

Argyle, M. (1978) 'Discussion chapter: an appraisal of the new approach to the study of social behaviour'. In M. Brenner, P. Marsh, and M. Brenner (eds), *The Social Contexts of Method*. London: Croom Helm.

Argyle, M., and Little, B. R. (1972) 'Do personality traits apply to social behaviour?' *Journal for the Theory of Social Behaviour*, 2, 1–35.

Argyle, M., Furnham, A., and Graham, J. A. (1981) *Social Situations*. Cambridge: Cambridge University Press.

Argyris, C. (1980) *Inner Contradictions of Rigorous Research*. New York: Academic Press.

Ariès, P. (1962) *Centuries of Childhood*. London: Cape.

Austin, J. L. (1962) *How to do Things with Words*. Oxford: Oxford University Press.

Averill, J. (1980) 'A constructivist theory of emotion'. In R. Plutchik and H. Kellermann, *Emotions: Theory, Research and Experience*. New York: Academic Press.

Backman, C. W. (1979) 'Epilogue: a new paradigm?' In G. P. Ginsberg (ed.), *Emerging Strategies in Social Psychological Research*. Chichester and New York: Wiley.

Bedford, E. (1957) 'Emotions'. *Proceedings of the Aristotelian Society*, 57, 281–304.

Bell, C. (1826) *Essays on the Anatomy of Expression in Painting*. London: Longman, Hurst, Rees and Orme.

Bower, T. G. R. (1982) *Development in Infancy*. 2nd edn. San Francisco, Calif.: Freeman.

Brenner, M. (1978) 'Interviewing'. In M. Brenner *et al.* (eds),   *The Social Context of Method*. London: Croom Helm.

Broadbent, D. (1981) 'Non-corporeal explanations in psychology'. In A. F. Heath (ed.), *Scientific Explanation*. Oxford: Clarendon Press.

Bruner, J. S. (1972) 'Visually pre-adapted constituents of manipulatory action'. *Perception*, 1, 3–14.

Bruner, J. S. (1983) *Children's Talk*. New York and London: Norton.

Bruner, J. S., and Garton, A. (1978) *Human Growth and Development*. Oxford: Clarendon.

Chomsky, N. (1965) *Aspects of the Theory of Syntax*. The Hague: Mouton.

Clarke, D. D. (1983) *Language and Action*. Oxford: Pergamon.

Collett, P., and Marsh, P. (1974) 'Patterns of public behaviour: collision avoidance on a pedestrian crossing'. *Semiotica*, 12, 281–99.

von Cranach, M. (1982) 'Ordinary interactive action: theory, methods and some empirical findings', with U. Kulbermatten. In M. von Cranach and R. Harré (eds), *The Analysis of Action*. Cambridge: Cambridge University Press.

Crowle, A. J. (1976) 'The deceptive language of laboratory'. In R. Harré (ed.), *Life Sentences*. Chichester: Wiley.

Darwin, C. (1859) *On the Origin of Species by Means of Natural Selection*. London: Murray.

Darwin, C. (1872) *The Expression of Emotion in Man and Animals*. London: Murray.

De Carlo, N. A. (1980) 'La quantificazione ovvero il numero come segnale'. *Psicologia Contemporanea*, 40.

De Carlo, N. A. (1983) *La scelta del campione*. Padua: Liviana.

Ekman, P. (1977) 'Biological and cultural contributions to body and facial movement'. In J. Blacking (ed.), *The Anthropology of the Body*. New York and London: Academic Press.

Eysenck, H. J. (1967) *Biological Basis of Personality*. Springfield, Ill.: C. Thomas.

Fodor, J. A. (1983) *Modularity of Mind*. Cambridge, Mass.: MIT Press.

Fransella, F., and Bannister, D. (1977) *A Manual for Repertory Grid Technique*. London: Academic Press.

Galbraith, J. K. (1977) *The Age of Uncertainty*. London: BBC and Deutsch.

Ginsberg, G. P. (ed.) (1979) *Emerging Strategies in Social Psychological Research*. Chichester and New York: Wiley.

Goffman, E. (1968) *Asylums*. Harmondsworth: Penguin.

Goffman, E. (1969) *The Presentation of Self in Everyday Life*. London: Allen Lane.

Gray, J. A. (1971) *The Psychology of Fear and Stress*. New York: McGraw-Hill.

Harré, R. (1979) *Social Being*. Oxford: Blackwell.

Harré, R. (1983) *Personal Being*. Oxford: Blackwell.

Harré, R., and Secord, P. F. (1972) *The Explanation of Social Behaviour*. Oxford: Blackwell.

Harré, R., and Waele, J.-P. de (1976) 'The ritual for incorporation of a stranger'. In R. Harré (ed.), *Life Sentence*. Chichester: Wiley.

Harris, R. (1980) *The Language Makers*. Oxford: Pergamon.

Heelas, P., and Lock, A. (1981) *Indigenous Psychologies*. London: Academic Press.

Helling, I. (1976) 'Autobiography as self-presentation'. In R. Harré (ed.), *Life Sentences*. Chichester: Wiley.

Ingleby, D. (1970) 'Ideology and the human sciences'. *Human Context*, 2, 159–80.

Jaspars, J., and Fraser, C. (1984) 'Attitudes and social representations'. In R. M. Farr and S. Moscovici (eds), *Social Representations*, chapter 3. Cambridge: Cambridge University Press.

Kaminsky, G. (1982) 'What beginner skiers can teach us about actions'. In M. von Cranach and R. Harré (eds), *The Analysis of Action*, 99–144. Cambridge: Cambridge University Press.

Kelly, G. A. (1955) *The Psychology of Personal Constructs*. New York: Norton.

Kohlberg, L. (1976) 'Moral stages and moralization: the cognitive-developmental approach'. In T. Lickona (ed.), *Moral Development and Behaviour*. New York: Holt, Rinehart & Winston.

Kreckel, M. (1981) *Communicative Acts and Shared Knowledge in Natural Discourse*. London: Academic Press.

Laing, R. D. (1967) *The Politics of Experience*. New York: Pantheon Books.

Leventhal, H. (1980) 'Towards a comprehensive theory of emotion'. In L. Berkowitz (ed.), *Advances in Experimental Social Psychology*, 13, 139 –207. New York: Academic Press.

Lévi-Strauss, C. (1968) *Structural Anthropology*. Trans. C. Jacobson and B. G. Schoepf. Harmondsworth: Penguin.

Lukes, S. (1973) *Individualism*. Oxford: Blackwell.

Lumsden, C. J., and Wilson, E. O. (1981) *Genes, Mind and Culture: The Coevolutionary Process*. Cambridge, Mass.: Harvard University Press.

Lutz, C. (1981) 'Situation based emotion frames and the cultural construction of emotions'. *Proceedings of IIIrd Annual Conference of the Cognitive Science Society*. Berkeley, Calif.

Margolis, J. (1984) *Philosophy of Psychology*. Englewood Cliffs, NJ: Prentice-Hall.

Marsh, P. (1978) *Aggro: The Illusion of Violence*. London: Dent.

Marsh, P., Rosser, E., and Harré, R. (1978) *The Rules of Disorder*. London: Routledge & Kegan Paul.

Marx, K., and Engels, F. (1973) *The German Ideology*. London: Lawrence & Wishart.

Michie, D. (1976) 'An advice-taking system for computer chess'. *Computer Bulletin,* 10 (ser. 2), 12–14.

Mischel, T. (1964) 'Personal constructs, rules and the logic of clinical activity'. *Psychological Review,* 71, 180–92.

Mixon, D. (1972) 'Instead of deception'. *Journal for the Theory of Social Behaviour,* 2, 145–77.

Morgan, J., O'Neill, C., and Harré, R. (1979) *Nicknames*. London: Routledge & Kegan Paul.

Morris, D. (1983) *Soccer Tribe*. London: Cape.

Morsbach, H. (1976) 'Amaeru'. In R. Harré (ed.), *Life Sentences*. Chichester: Wiley.

Namboodiri, N. K. (1978) *Survey Sampling and Measurement*. New York: Academic Press.

Needham, R. (1972) *Belief, Language and Experience*. Oxford: Blackwell.

Nisbett, R. E., and Wilson, T. D. (1977) 'Telling more than we can know: verbal reports on mental processes'. *Psychological Review,* 84, 231–59.

O'Neill, J. (1972) *Modes of Individualism and Collectivism*. London: Heinemann.

Pearce, B., and Cronen, V. (1980) *Communication, Action and Meaning*. New York: Praeger.

Pendleton, D. A., and Hasler, J. D. (1983) *Doctor–Patient Communication*. London: Academic Press.

Piaget, J. (1932) *The Moral Judgement of the Child*, chapter 1. London: Routledge & Kegan Paul.

Pliner, P., Blackstein, K., and Spiegel, J. (1975) *The Perception of the Emotions in the Self and Others*. New York: Academic Press.

Plutchik, R. (1980) *Emotion: A Psychoevolutionary Synthesis*. London: Harper & Row.

Powers, W. T. (1973) *Behaviour: The Control of Perception*. Chicago, Ill.: Aldine.

Rosser, E., and Harré, R. (1976) 'The meaning of "trouble"'. In M. Hammersley and P. Woods (eds), *The Process of Schooling*, chapter 20. London: Routledge & Kegan Paul.

Rosser, E., and Harré, R. (1977) 'Explicit knowledge of personal style'. *Journal for the Theory of Social Behaviour,* 7, 249–51.

Sabini, J., and Silver, M. (1982) *Moralities of Everyday Life*. New York: Oxford University Press.

Saussure, F. de (1974) *Course in General Linguistics*. Trans. Wade Baskin. London: Fontana and Collins.

Schachter, S. (1971) *Emotion, Obesity and Crime*. New York: Academic Press.

Schank, R. C. (1982) *Dynamic Memory: A Theory of Reminding and Learning in Computers and People*. Cambridge: Cambridge University Press.

Schank, R. C., and Abelson, R. P. (1977) *Scripts, Plans, Goals and Understanding*. Hillsdale, NJ: Erlbaum.

Segl, H., and Bauer, W. (1975) *Forschung-Methoden der Psychologie*. Stuttgart: Kohlhammer.

Shaw, M. L. G. (ed.) (1980) *Recent Advances in Personal Construct Theory*. London: Academic Press.

Shotter, J., and Newson, J. (1982) 'An ecological approach to cognitive development: implacate orders, joint action and intentionality'. In J. Butterworth and P. Light (eds), *Social Cognition: Studies of the Development of Understanding*. Brighton: Harvester.

Simon, H. A. (1981) *The Sciences of the Artificial*. 2nd edn. Cambridge, Mass.: MIT Press.

Sluckin, A. (1981) *Growing Up in the Playground: The Social Development of Children*. London: Routledge & Kegan Paul.

Sudman, S. (1976) *Applied Sampling*. New York: Academic Press.

Totman, R. (1985) *Psychology as Deception* (forthcoming).

Turner, J. (1980) 'Fairness or discrimination in intergroup behaviour?' *European Journal of Social Psychology*, 10, 131–46.

Veblen, T. (1899) *A Theory of the Leisure Class*. New York: Macmillan Company.

Volpato, C. (1982) *Sviluppi della teoria etogenica del comportamento sociale*. Bologna: Patron.

Vygotsky, L. (1962) *Thought and Language*. Cambridge, Mass.: MIT Press.

de Waele, J.-P., and Harré, R. (1977) 'The personality of individuals'. In R. Harré (ed.), *Personality*. Oxford: Blackwell.

de Waele, J.-P., and Harré, R. (1979) 'Autobiography as a psychological method'. In G. P. Ginsberg (ed.), *Emerging Strategies in Social Psychological Research*. Chichester and New York: Wiley.

Wittgenstein, L. (1980) *Remarks on the Foundations of Psychology*, vols I and II. Trans. G. E. M. Anscombe, C. G. Luckhardt and M. A. E. Anne. Oxford: Blackwell.

Wood, L. (1983) 'Loneliness'. In R. Harré and R. Lamb (eds), *The Encyclopedic Dictionary of Psychology*. Oxford: Blackwell.

Woods, W. A. (1970) 'Transition network grammars for natural language'. *Communications of the ACM*, 13, 591–606.

Yardley, K. (1982) 'On engaging actors in as-if experiments'. *Journal for the Theory of Social Behaviour*, 12, 291–304.

FURTHER READING

Chapman, A. J., and Jones, D. M. (eds) (1980) *Models of Man*. Leicester: British Psychological Society.
Coulter, J. (1981) *The Social Construction of Mind*. London: Macmillan.
Gergen, K. J. (1982) *Towards Transformation in Social Knowledge*. New York: Springer-Verlag.
Hesse, M. B. (1966) *Models and Analogies in Science*. London: Sheed & Ward.
Hudson, L. (1972) *The Cult of the Fact*. London: Cape.
Shotter, J. (1984) *Social Accountability and Selfhood*. Oxford: Blackwell.
Wilshire, B. (1982) *Role Playing and Identity*. Bloomington, Ind.: Indiana University Press.

INDEX OF NAMES

INDEX OF SUBJECTS

syndromes, mental, 70
syntagmatic axis, 102–3

theoretical terms: meaning of, 47;
role of, 48–9
theories: nature of, 42–7; as co-
ordinated models, 44–7;
testability, 48–9

topic domain, 61–2, 64
transformation explanation, 51
type v. token, 84

universalism, 2, 7–9

'why' questions, laddering of, 29